SRA Open Court Reading

Grade 3 • Book 1

Themes

- Respect
- Extreme Weather
- A Changing Nation

Mc
Graw
Hill
Education

Acknowledgments

Grateful acknowledgment is given to the following publishers and copyright owners for permissions granted to reprint selections from their publications. All possible care has been taken to trace ownership and secure permission for each selection included. In case of any errors or omissions, the Publisher will be pleased to make suitable acknowledgments in future editions.

Respect

THE ORIGAMI MASTER. Text copyright ©2008 by Nathaniel Lachenmeyer, Illustrations copyright ©2008 by Aki Sogabe. Published in 2008 by Albert Whitman & Company.

"Language of the Birds" from A MOVIE IN MY PILLOW by Jorge Argueta, illustrated by Elizabeth Gómez. Text Copyright ©2007 by Jorge Argueta. Illustrations Copyright ©2007 by Elizabeth Gómez. Permission arranged with LEE & LOW BOOKS, Inc., New York, NY 10016. All rights not specifically granted herein are reserved.

"My Grandma's Stories" from A MOVIE IN MY PILLOW by Jorge Argueta, illustrated by Elizabeth Gómez. Text Copyright ©2007 by Jorge Argueta. Illustrations Copyright ©2007 by Elizabeth Gómez. Permission arranged with LEE & LOW BOOKS, Inc., New York, NY 10016. All rights not specifically granted herein are reserved.

Jim by Gwendolyn Brooks. Reprinted by consent of Brooks Permissions.

THE PRAIRIE FIRE. Text Copyright Marilynn Reynolds, illustrations copyright Don Kilby. Used with the permission of Orca Book Publishers Ltd.

The White Spider's Gift by Jamie Turner is reprinted with the permission of the publisher Plays, The Drama Magazine for Young People/Sterling Partners Inc.

Extreme Weather

TORNADOES! by Gail Gibbons. Used by permission of Holiday House Publishers.

Winter Dance by Linda Kao, illustrated by Maria Mola; from Ladybug Magazine, January 2013. Copyright © by Carus Publishing Company. Reproduced with permission. All Cricket Media material is copyrighted by Carus Publishing Company, d/b/a Cricket Media, and/or various authors and illustrators. Any commercial use or distribution of material without permission is strictly prohibited. Please visit http://www.cricketmedia.com/info/licensing2 for licensing and http://www.cricketmedia.com for subscriptions.

Spring Wind by Lucy Ford, illustrated by Julia Sarcone-Roach; from Ladybug Magazine, March 2012. Copyright © by Carus Publishing Company. Reproduced with permission. All Cricket Media material is copyrighted by Carus Publishing Company, d/b/a Cricket Media, and/or various authors and illustrators. Any commercial use or distribution of material without permission is strictly prohibited. Please visit http://www.cricketmedia.com/info/licensing2 for licensing and http://www.cricketmedia.com for subscriptions.

Einstein Anderson: The Hurricane Hoax by Seymour Simon. Copyright ©2013 by Seymour Simon. Used by permission of StarWalk Kids Media.

A Changing Nation

"The Dream Keeper" by Langston Hughes. Reprinted by permission of Harold Ober Associates Incorporated.

"My People" by Langston Hughes. Reprinted by permission of Harold Ober Associates Incorporated.

"Words Like Freedom" by Langston Hughes. Reprinted by permission of Harold Ober Associates Incorporated.

"The Dream Keeper," "My People," and "Words Like Freedom" from THE COLLECTED POEMS OF LANGSTON HUGHES by Langston Hughes, edited by Arnold Rampersad with David Roessel, Alfred A. Knopf, an imprint of Knopf Doubleday Publishing Group, a division of Random House LLC. All rights reserved.

The Dancing Bird of Paradise by Renee S. Sanford, from Cricket Magazine, November 2001.

Arbor Day Square by Kathryn O. Galbraith. First published in the United States under the title Arbor Day Square by Kathryn O. Galbraith, illustrated by Cyd Moore. Text Copyright© 2010 by Kathryn O. Galbraith. Illustrations Copyright© 2010 by Cyd Moore. Published by arrangement with Peachtree Publishers. All rights reserved.

MHEonline.com

Send all inquiries to:
McGraw-Hill Education
8787 Orion Place
Columbus, OH 43240

ISBN: 978-0-02-135403-0
MHID: 0-02-135403-0

Printed in the United States of America

2 3 4 5 6 7 8 9 LWI 21 20 19 18 17

Program Authors

Carl Bereiter, Ph.D.
Professor Emeritus at the Ontario Institute for Studies in Education, University of Toronto

Andrew Biemiller, Ph.D.
Professor Emeritus at the Institute of Child Study, University of Toronto

Joe Campione, Ph.D.
Professor Emeritus in the Graduate School of Education at the University of California, Berkeley

Doug Fuchs, Ph.D.
Nicholas Hobbs Professor of Special Education and Human Development at Vanderbilt University

Lynn Fuchs, Ph.D.
Nicholas Hobbs Professor of Special Education and Human Development at Vanderbilt University

Steve Graham, Ph.D.
Mary Emily Warner Professor in the Mary Lou Fulton Teachers College at Arizona State University

Karen Harris, Ph.D.
Mary Emily Warner Professor in the Mary Lou Fulton Teachers College at Arizona State University

Jan Hirshberg, Ed.D.
Reading and writing consultant in Alexandria, Virginia

Anne McKeough, Ph.D.
Professor Emeritus in the Division of Applied Psychology at the University of Calgary

Marsha Roit, Ed.D.
Reading curricula expert and professional development consultant

Marlene Scardamalia, Ph.D.
Presidents' Chair in Education and Knowledge Technologies at the University of Toronto

Marcy Stein, Ph.D.
Professor and founding member of the Education Program at the University of Washington, Tacoma

Gerald H. Treadway Jr, Ph.D.
Professor Emeritus, School of Education at San Diego State University

In memory of our friend and colleague,
Daniel Wendell, Grade 3 Editor

Getting Started

UNIT 1

Respect

UNIT 3

A Changing Nation

Genre Adventure Tale

Essential Question
What if something unexpected happens while you are looking for an adventure?

Robinson Crusoe

by Daniel Defoe
adapted and retold by Vidas Barzdukas
illustrated by Ryan Durney

All my life I craved adventure. My parents wanted me to stay home in England. Yet I wanted to be a sailor. I dreamed of sailing across the ocean and visiting faraway places. My biggest adventure was when I was shipwrecked on a deserted island.

It began when our ship sailed into a fierce storm. As we neared an island, the ship hit a sandbar. We were stuck! Powerful waves began tearing the ship to pieces. We tried to row a smaller boat to the island. Then a large wave rolled the boat over and threw us overboard. I was done for, I thought! However, the ship's dog and I managed to swim ashore and collapse in the sand. Little did I know that I was the only human to survive....

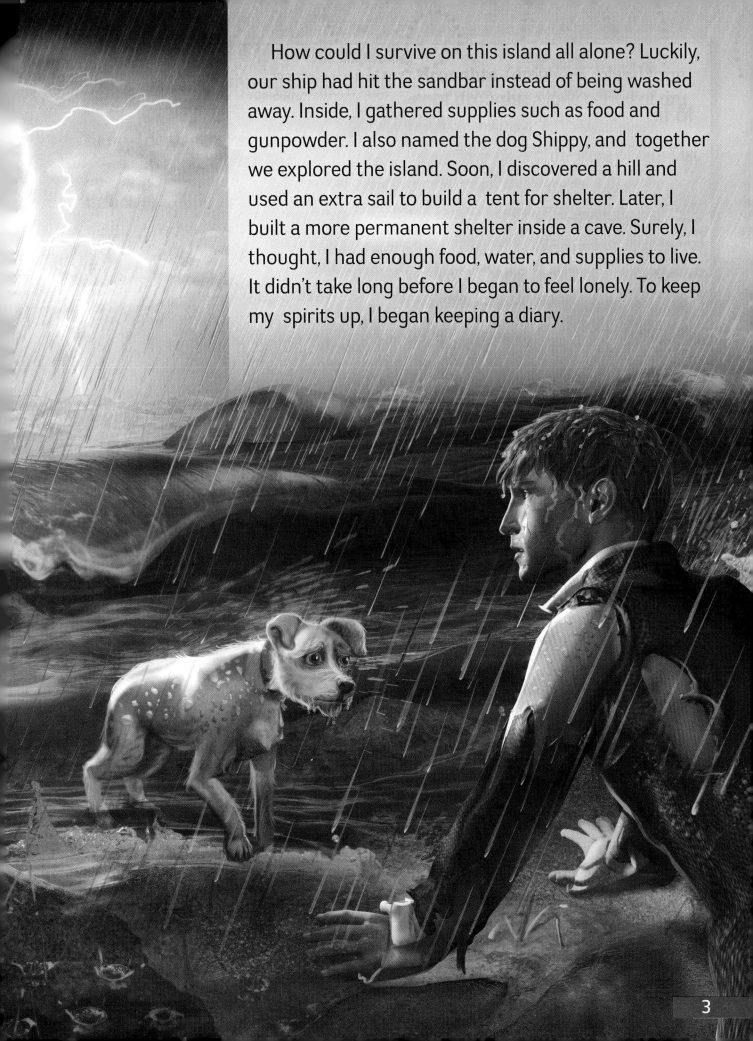

How could I survive on this island all alone? Luckily, our ship had hit the sandbar instead of being washed away. Inside, I gathered supplies such as food and gunpowder. I also named the dog Shippy, and together we explored the island. Soon, I discovered a hill and used an extra sail to build a tent for shelter. Later, I built a more permanent shelter inside a cave. Surely, I thought, I had enough food, water, and supplies to live. It didn't take long before I began to feel lonely. To keep my spirits up, I began keeping a diary.

Each day was the same routine. In the morning, I hunted for food or tended the crops. In the afternoon, I napped. At sunset, I made dinner and worked around the shelter. After a while, I became very good at carving bowls and making candles.

Every morning, Shippy and I walked around the island, too. As we walked, I told Shippy about my life and my adventures. He was a good companion and a great listener. Shippy and I made a new friend on the island. He was a parrot that I named Poll. I felt like the island was finally becoming a home.

One day, I became very sick. There was nobody to care for me as I lay in my shelter. I missed my home and parents terribly. *Why hadn't I stayed home? Why did I leave my family to go on an adventure?* I tried to take comfort in my companions, Shippy and Poll. Eventually, I started to feel better, and after several days, the fever passed.

Before I knew it, several years had passed.
I grew crops and fruit trees. And after finding a
family of wild goats, I was able to start my own
flock. The goats provided me with milk and meat.
I also wore clothes made from goat skins with a
big, floppy hat. I wonder what my family and friends
would have thought!

Then one day, I made a startling discovery.
I found a footprint in the sand. And it wasn't mine!
I immediately ran back to my shelter and hid. *What
if someone found me? Would they take me away
from the island?*

Then one evening, I came across several natives
on the beach. They were building a fire. I watched
them from afar. Every morning I returned to the
beach to see if the natives returned. They did not
return for many years.

One night, I heard a cannon boom in the distance. Was a ship in danger? The next morning, I found a ship dashed against the rocks. I couldn't find the crew, so I assumed they drowned in the shipwreck. However, I found another dog from that ship and I named him Scruffy.

Months later, I saw that the natives had returned. This time they had a prisoner. I helped the prisoner escape and hid him in my cave. I asked the prisoner his name, but he did not speak English. So I called him Friday because that was the day we met. We did not speak the same language, but we became good friends.

For the next three years, Friday and I lived and worked together. We hunted in the morning and worked on the farm in the afternoon. I learned that Friday had once left home for adventure, too, just like me.

One morning, a ship appeared and dropped off three prisoners on the beach. I learned that one of the prisoners was the captain of the ship. The crew had mutinied! Friday and I helped the captain get his ship back. In return, the captain sailed Friday and me back to England. I had been on this island for more than twenty-eight years!

Read this Social Studies Connection. You will answer the questions as a class.

Text Feature

A **caption** tells about a picture and adds information to an article or story.

The History of Ships

People have used ships for thousands of years. The first ships were rafts made of logs. These logs were tied together with vines. Later, sailors used oars to move ships through the water. Some early ships also used sails. These sails were large pieces of cloth tied to a tall pole called a mast. When the sails caught the wind, the ship was pulled forward.

Many changes in ships have happened over the years. The first big change was the steam engine replacing the sail. Like the sail, it helped ships move faster. One ship that used steam power was the paddle steamer. On a paddle steamer, giant blades plunge into the water to push the boat. Later, the blades were replaced by propellers. Unlike the blades on the paddle boat, propeller blades spin around like fan blades.

Most modern ships are made out of steel. These ships do not use wind or steam power. Instead, they use gas or diesel fuel to power the engines. Some steel ships even use alternative forms of power. What will ships be like in the future?

The first paddle steamer appeared back in the late 1700s.

1. What new information did you learn from the caption?

2. Why is the past important to us today?

3. How has the world changed and how might it change in the future?

 Go Digital

Do some research to find out how changes in ships have affected their speed. How fast can paddle steamers travel? How fast can gas powered ships with propellers travel?

BIG Idea

What does *respect* mean to you?

Theme Connections

How are these people showing respect?

 Background Builder Video
connected.mcgraw-hill.com

11

Genre Fantasy

Essential Questions
How important is friendship? Why should you respect and support your friends?

12

The Origami Master

by Nathaniel Lachenmeyer
illustrated by Aki Sogabe

Shima the Origami Master lived alone, high up in the mountains. He never had visitors. His origami kept him company.

One day, a warbler chose the tree in Shima's backyard for its nest. It flew back and forth, collecting twigs.

When the warbler was done for the day, it sat on a branch and watched Shima doing origami. From time to time, it sang: "Hoohokekyo... hoohokekyo."

That evening, after Shima went to bed, the warbler flew in through the open doorway and alighted on his desk. It began to fold a piece of paper the way it had seen Shima do.

The next morning, Shima discovered a new paper elephant on his desk. He picked it up and examined it closely. It was simpler and more beautiful than any of the ones he had made. Someone is playing a trick on me, he thought.

Shima threw his elephants away. He decided
to make a dragon. In his opinion, his origami
dragons were the best in the world.

In the morning, Shima found a magnificent
new dragon on his desk. It looked like it was
about to come to life and fly back to its lair.

Shima spent the day folding origami spiders. At dusk, he left his best spider on his desk. Then, he hid in the hall. He was determined to find out who was making the origami.

In the middle of the night, the warbler flew inside and began making an origami spider. Shima watched in amazement. He decided to try to catch the warbler and learn its secrets.

Just after sunrise, Shima hiked down the
mountain to the city below.

He bought a large birdcage and a lock, and
returned home.

That night, Shima hid under his desk. When the warbler arrived, he caught it and put it in the cage.

The warbler cried and beat its wings against the cage, but it could not escape.

Shima brought the warbler his best origami paper. He gathered nuts and berries for it to eat.

But the warbler just stared sadly at the tree, where its nest was waiting.

Shima stayed up all night, making every origami animal he could think of. The warbler did not look at any of them. Finally, as the sun rose in the sky, Shima fell asleep.

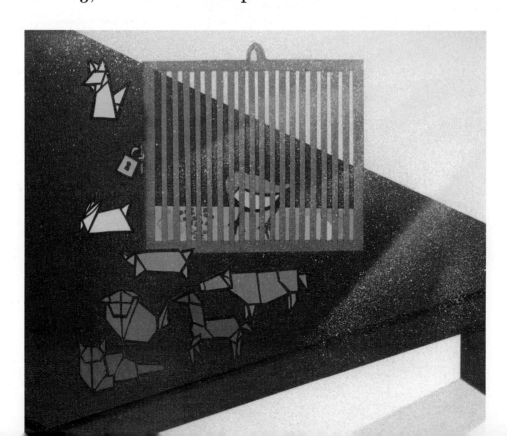

When Shima woke up, he found the cage door
open and the warbler gone. The lock was lying
next to the cage. Beside it was an origami key.

Shima ran outside. The warbler's nest was empty. It made Shima sad to think that he had scared the bird away. Then, he saw the warbler returning to the tree with a twig in its beak. He smiled when he heard its beautiful song: "Hoohokekyo… hoohokekyo."

Shima realized how much he would miss the
warbler if it left. He sat down and began work on
something new—an origami nest for the friend he
had made and almost lost.

Comprehension

Text Connections

1. What makes Shima an origami master?

2. Do you think that Shima is lonely? Use evidence from the text to explain why.

3. Is Shima or the warbler a greater master of origami? Describe how the actions of each character help you decide your answer.

4. How does Shima show respect for the warbler in the end? Think about how you would have treated the warbler compared to how Shima did.

Did You Know?

The Japanese bush warbler is a real bird that is very shy. It stays hidden in leaves during the day. Because of its beautiful singing, many people keep them in cages.

Look Closer

Keys to Comprehension

1. What makes the warbler's origami better than Shima's?

2. What characteristics does the warbler have that make it able to create beautiful origami?

Writer's Craft

3. What is another way of saying, "Someone is playing a trick on me," from page 17?

Concept Development

4. What does the picture of the key next to the cage tell you about the warbler?

5. Nathaniel Lachenmeyer wrote the book *Scarlatti's Cat*. It's about a great composer of music and his cat, who has a gift for music. How is that plot similar to "The Origami Master"?

Write

Would you try to tame a wild bird? Write a story about how you would or would not try to tame a wild bird, and why.

Vocabulary Words

- **alighted**
- **amazement**
- **dusk**
- **evening**
- **examined**
- **forth**
- **lair**
- **magnificent**
- **master**
- **opinion**
- **origami**
- **warbler**

A Concert to Remember

Sunday night at dusk, the Little Walnut Elementary School Orchestra and Choir performed a spring concert. The setting was outdoors in the park behind the school. Just before the sun started to set, the musicians came forth to take their seats and tune their instruments. People streamed in and sat on blankets in the grass, eager to see the show. It was quite a crowd; even songbirds seemed to alight onto tree branches to listen. The conductor moved in, and with a swish of the baton, the music began.

Familiar works of the masters, including Mozart, Beethoven, and Bach, were played magnificently. The conductor mixed in some current songs as well. It was hard to believe the notes were coming from musicians so young. The concert ended with Brahm's Lullaby. It was as if a flock of warblers had come from their lair to delight the listeners.

In my humble opinion, this concert was as fine as any professional performance I have seen. Many listeners actually examined the stage to make sure there were no signs of a recording. They were amazed to find hundreds of origami cranes littering the stage. The conductor had given them to the musicians for good luck. It seems to have worked.

As the musicians packed up their instruments, the crowd let out a loud cheer. It was our way of saying thank you for a splendid evening and BRAVO!

Concept Vocabulary

Think about the word *compassion*. When has somebody shown you compassion?

Extend Vocabulary

Copy the words below into your Writer's Notebook. Then write the vocabulary word that means about the same as each set of examples.

great, wonderful, stupendous _____

looked, saw, observed _____

surprise, shock, astonishment _____

pro, star, expert _____

Read this Science Connection. You will answer the questions as a class.

Text Feature

Parentheses are placed around words that add information.

Designing a Solution

In "The Origami Master," the warbler creates a paper key that is able to unlock the cage door. The warbler designed a solution to his problem that allowed him to escape. He was able to use the materials he had been given and had a limited amount of time to work as his captor was sleeping.

You can solve simple design problems, too, using materials that are available to you. You do this if you create something that stops a table or chair from wobbling. You do this if you create a patch for something that has been torn or broken.

Look around for problems that you can solve by engineering a simple design using materials you have.

1. Examine the problem (inspect the problem to see what is causing it).

2. Decide what needs to be solved and how it will work once it is solved.

3. Look for materials you have on hand. Do you have all the materials you need? What else might you need (paper, tissue, cloth, books, crayons)?

4. Test your solutions (try different ways to see which one works best).

1. What are some examples of simple problems that you can fix by designing a solution using materials from your classroom?

2. Look at the illustration of possible classroom materials you could use to fix a problem. What are some other materials you could use that are not illustrated above?

3. What is a problem you could not fix with classroom materials? How could you fix it? What materials would you need, how long would it take, and what would it cost?

 Go Digital

Search for tips or videos on fixing the problem you selected. You might get some good ideas.

Essential Questions
What can learning about your heritage teach you about yourself? How can you have fun by trying new things?

Don Viet Barber

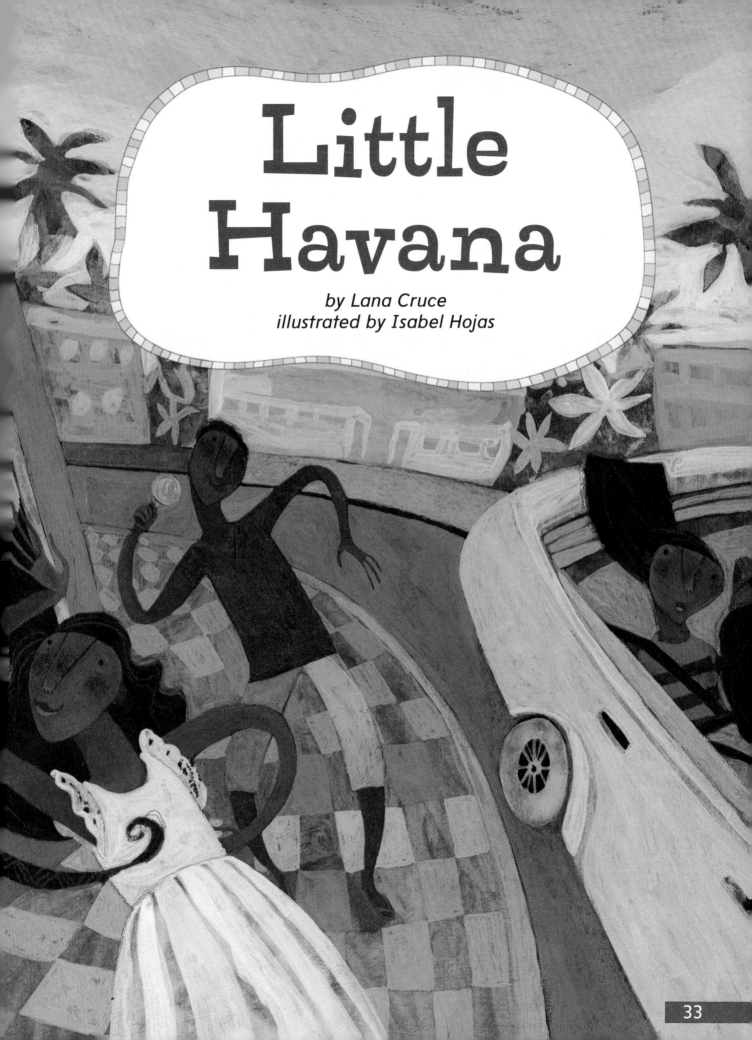

Little Havana

by Lana Cruce
illustrated by Isabel Hojas

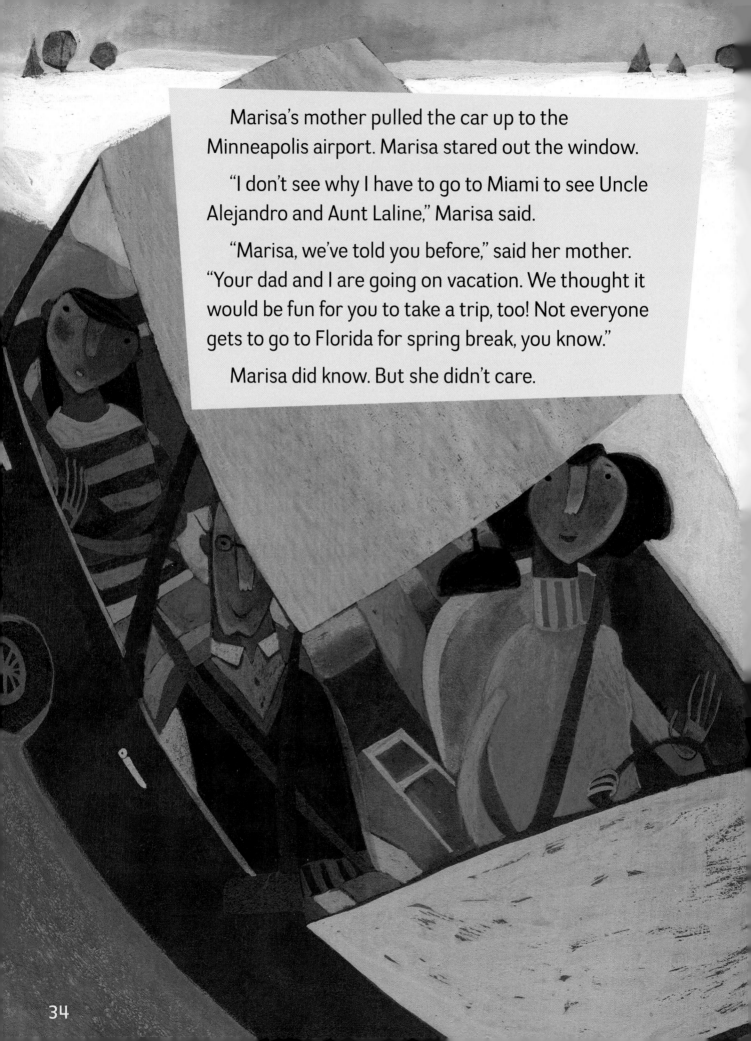

Marisa's mother pulled the car up to the Minneapolis airport. Marisa stared out the window.

"I don't see why I have to go to Miami to see Uncle Alejandro and Aunt Laline," Marisa said.

"Marisa, we've told you before," said her mother. "Your dad and I are going on vacation. We thought it would be fun for you to take a trip, too! Not everyone gets to go to Florida for spring break, you know."

Marisa did know. But she didn't care.

Marisa slumped in the seat. Once in Miami, she would be all alone with her aunt and uncle. She had never met them before.

"You're going to love Miami, Marisa," her mother said.

"Uncle Alejandro and Aunt Laline are from Cuba," Marisa's father said from the front seat. "We want you to meet some of your Cuban relatives."

"They live in a cool neighborhood called Little Havana," said her father. "Just like the city in Cuba called Havana. The city of Miami is only about 230 miles from there."

"It may be the closest you ever get to visiting the land of our ancestors," said Marisa's mother.

"I don't even know them," Marisa muttered.

A few hours later, Marisa's flight arrived in
Miami. Marisa grabbed her bags and left the plane.
When she stepped into the airport, she was surprised.
There were so many people! She couldn't find anybody
she recognized.

How will I know Uncle Alejandro and Aunt Laline?
Marisa thought unhappily.

Just then, Marisa noticed a man and a woman
waving at her. They were holding a big sign that read
"Marisa, *la hermosa.*"

What does that mean? Marisa wondered. She felt
her stomach drop. She didn't know much Spanish.
*How can I have fun if I don't even understand their
language?* she thought. She wished she was back in
Minneapolis with her friends.

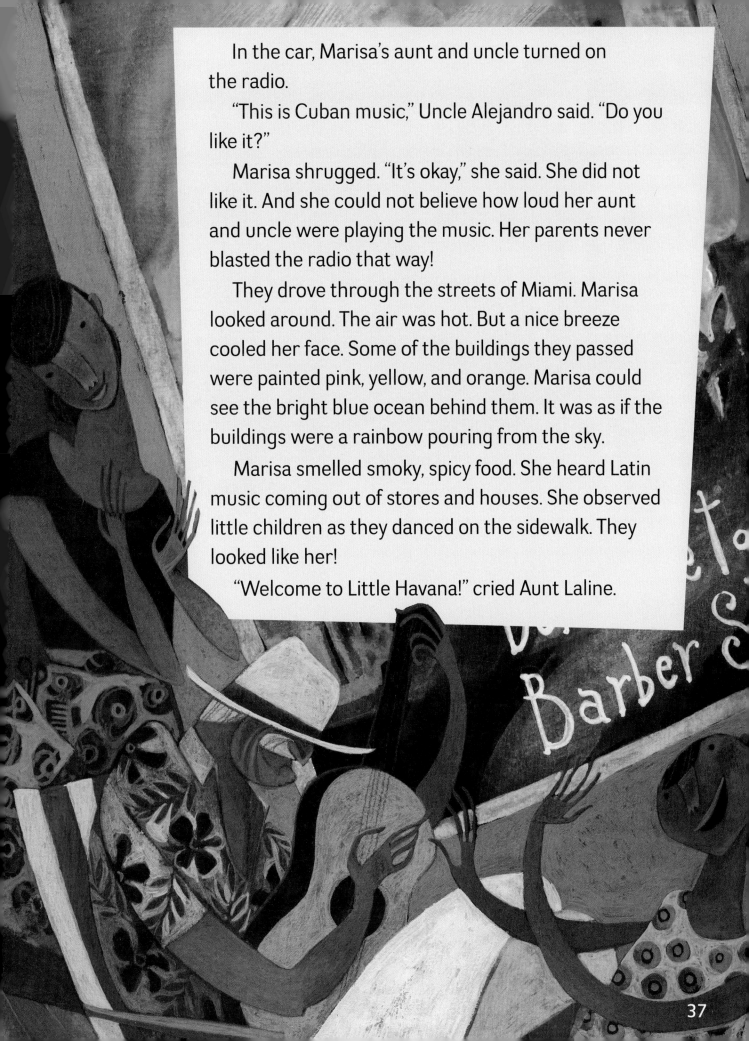

In the car, Marisa's aunt and uncle turned on the radio.

"This is Cuban music," Uncle Alejandro said. "Do you like it?"

Marisa shrugged. "It's okay," she said. She did not like it. And she could not believe how loud her aunt and uncle were playing the music. Her parents never blasted the radio that way!

They drove through the streets of Miami. Marisa looked around. The air was hot. But a nice breeze cooled her face. Some of the buildings they passed were painted pink, yellow, and orange. Marisa could see the bright blue ocean behind them. It was as if the buildings were a rainbow pouring from the sky.

Marisa smelled smoky, spicy food. She heard Latin music coming out of stores and houses. She observed little children as they danced on the sidewalk. They looked like her!

"Welcome to Little Havana!" cried Aunt Laline.

Uncle Alejandro and Aunt Laline's apartment was bright and cheerful. There was a palm tree outside. You could almost touch it from their balcony.

"You got here just in time for the *Calle Ocho* Festival, *sobrina*," said Aunt Laline.

"What is the *Calle Ocho* Festival?" Marisa asked.

"*Calle Ocho* means 'Eighth Street' in Spanish," said Uncle Alejandro. "It's a big party that happens every March on Eighth Street."

"Many people come together to have fun. They also learn about and experience Cuban culture," said Aunt Laline.

I am not looking forward to this, Marisa thought.

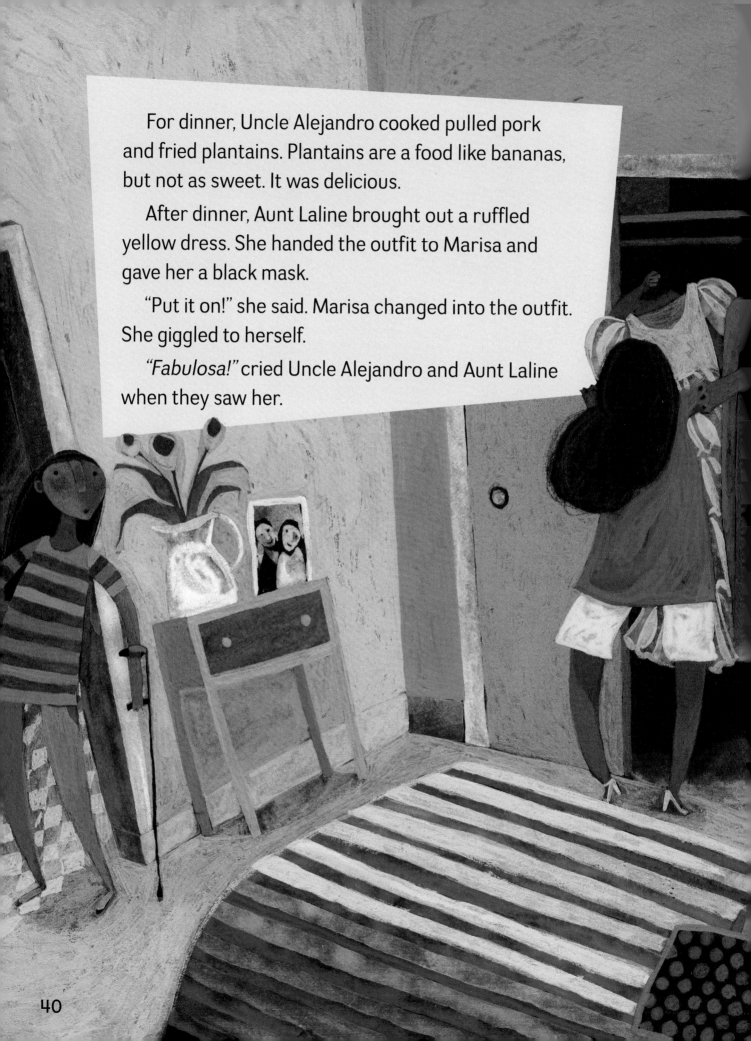

For dinner, Uncle Alejandro cooked pulled pork and fried plantains. Plantains are a food like bananas, but not as sweet. It was delicious.

After dinner, Aunt Laline brought out a ruffled yellow dress. She handed the outfit to Marisa and gave her a black mask.

"Put it on!" she said. Marisa changed into the outfit. She giggled to herself.

"Fabulosa!" cried Uncle Alejandro and Aunt Laline when they saw her.

Marisa peered in the mirror. She had to try hard not to grin. She loved the outfit. She didn't want to admit that she was having a lot of fun.

"Tomorrow you'll wear the costume to *Calle Ocho!*" said Aunt Laline.

Marisa stared at her aunt in shock.

"Oh no!" she cried. "I can't do that!"

"Why not?" asked Uncle Alejandro.

"I can't parade down the street wearing this," said Marisa. "No way!" Marisa always wore jeans. She could never wear this frilly thing in public.

The next morning, Marisa woke up to a yummy smell.

"Café con leche," Uncle Alejandro explained. Marisa tasted a tiny amount. The coffee was strong but sweet.

After breakfast, Uncle Alejandro and Aunt Laline put on their costumes.

"Are you sure you don't want to wear yours?" asked Aunt Laline.

"I'm sure," Marisa said. She didn't want to stick out in the crowd.

They walked out into the street. A sea of people had already gathered.

43

Calle Ocho was like nothing Marisa had ever seen. Bands played. People mingled and marched. Everywhere people of all ages were dancing. They were all wearing beautiful, elaborate costumes. Marisa felt sad that she hadn't worn her yellow dress. She remembered looking in the mirror at the elegant dress.

"Aunt Laline," Marisa said, tugging on her aunt's dress. "Can I go back upstairs and put on the yellow dress?"

Her aunt's face broke into a big smile. "Of course you can!" she said.

Marisa hugged her. "I'm so happy I came to visit you!" she cried.

That night, after they went home, Marisa was exhausted. Outside she could still hear the sounds of the party going on. She called her mom and dad on the phone.

"I'm having so much fun," she told them.

"We knew you would, *hija*," they said.

Language of the Birds

by Jorge Argueta
illustrated by Elizabeth Gómez

I used to speak
only Spanish

Now I can speak
English too

And in my dreams
I speak in Nahuatl

the language
my grandma says

her people
—the Pipiles—

learned
from the birds

The Pipiles are an indigenous people of El Salvador who speak Nahuatl, the language of the Aztecs.

46

My Grandma's Stories

by Jorge Argueta
illustrated by Elizabeth Gómez

*I call my grandma "Mita"—an affectionate
term for "mi abuelita" ("my grandma")*

Mita's stories
filled her shack
with stars

Mita's stories
put smiles
on our faces

Mita's stories
are old
like the mountains

Mita's stories
are like the songs
of the crickets

If I close my eyes
I hear them
in the wind

You will answer the comprehension questions on these pages as a class.

Text Connections

1. What are three differences among the Cuban people's lives in Minneapolis and those in Little Havana? Give specific examples from the text.

2. What changes Marisa's mind about Little Havana?

3. What do the two poems and the story have in common?

4. How is Marisa like Shima in "The Origami Master"?

Did You Know?

Spanish is spoken throughout Mexico and in most of Central and South America. Nahuatl is the language of the ancient Aztecs. Today over one million people in Central Mexico still speak Nahuatl.

Look Closer

Keys to Comprehension

1. How does Marisa come to appreciate and respect her relatives who live in Little Havana?

2. How does the speaker in the poems show that he loves and respects his grandmother?

Writer's Craft

3. When the speaker in "My Grandma's Stories" says, "Mita's stories filled her shack with stars," what does it mean?

4. At the beginning of the story, how does Marisa feel about going on a trip to visit her relatives? How do you think you would feel if you had the same opportunity?

Concept Development

5. How are the poems "Language of the Birds" and "My Grandma's Stories" the same? How are they different?

Write

Write down a story that one of your relatives told you. You might want to start a book of their stories.

**Read this text.
Then discuss it
with your class.**

Vocabulary Words

- **ancestors**
- **elaborate**
- **elegant**
- **exhausted**
- **experience**
- **frilly**
- **mingled**
- **muttered**
- **parade**
- **peered**
- **recognized**
- **tasted**

A Beautiful Wedding

Imagine that you have been invited to an elegant party for the wedding of one of your relatives. It is quite the rare opportunity. Here is what you might see when you attend:

All the guests will be wearing fancy clothes. Traditionally, men wear a suit and tie. Many of the women wear dresses. The bride will be joined by bridesmaids. Bridesmaids are friends who help the bride during the wedding. They often wear identical frilly dresses.

When the bride walks down the aisle, she will parade before the attendants. Music will play. The bride will be wearing a fancy and stylish dress. When she walks, everybody will peer at her from their seats. She will be the center of attention.

The reception will have amazing decorations and plenty of food. When you taste the food, it will probably be delicious. Often times, the bride and groom have worked with a wedding planner to organize their wedding. Even with the help of the wedding planner, they still spend many hours making elaborate preparations.

Guests will mingle. Some of the guests have come from far away to attend the wedding. You may meet many family members you have not met before. Sometimes, they are only related through distant relatives. When you talk with them, speak clearly and do not mutter. You want to be recognized as an outstanding member of the family.

You might want to ask some of your family members about some of the things that happened during the ceremony. Often times, people do things their ancestors did a long time ago.

At the end of the wedding, you may be exhausted, but you will have experienced a night to remember.

Concept Vocabulary

Think about the word *appreciation*. What are ways you can show appreciation to somebody who invites you to a party?

Extend Vocabulary

Copy the words below into your Writer's Notebook. Then write the vocabulary word that shares a base with each pair of examples.

ancestry, ancestral _____

elaboration, elaborately _____

experiencing, experienced _____

tasty, tasteless _____

recognizable, recognizably _____

Different Cultures

In "Little Havana," Marisa travels to Miami, Florida, to visit her Cuban relatives. Her parents are Cuban too, but they live in Minnesota. Her parents tell her that it may be "the closest you ever get to visiting the land of our ancestors."

Cuba is an island country 90 miles to the south of Florida, in the Caribbean Sea. In the 1950s, there was a revolution in Cuba and the government changed. Many people fled Cuba for the United States. Of these refugees, many came from Havana, Cuba's capital and largest city. When Cuban refugees arrived in the U.S., a large number settled in Miami, where they formed a Cuban neighborhood. They named their new neighborhood Little Havana. They had no plans to return to the home of their ancestors.

The immigrants brought their culture with them. The food, the music, the clothes, language, and religion that they had in Cuba came to Little Havana.

Marisa experiences many new things while visiting Little Havana. Compare and contrast your culture with that of Marisa's relatives. What experiences would be new to you? What would be familiar?

At the *Calle Ocho* festival, many people celebrate Cuban heritage by waving that country's flag in parades.

1. How did the Cuban refugees that settled in Miami show their respect for the home of their ancestors?

2. How does the caption add information about the picture above?

3. What are some similarities between your culture and the culture of Marisa's relatives in Little Havana? What are some differences?

 Go Digital

Search for *Little Havana* and *Calle Ocho* to see pictures that show the Cuban culture. Compare what you find to pictures of Havana, Cuba. Find other Little Havanas in the United States. Do you see the same types of food, buildings, clothes, and festivals?

Genre Legend

Essential Questions

How important is trust between friends? Have you ever worked hard to show somebody that you care about him or her? What would you be willing to give up for a friend?

DAMON
AND
PYTHIAS

by Brian Dalton
illustrated by Stephanie Bisacco

SYRACUSE

Damon and Pythias were the best of friends. As children, the boys enjoyed running races against each other. Both of them were very fast and competitive, and both wanted to win. However, when they weren't competing, they cheered for each other. When Damon won a race, Pythias was happy for his friend. When Pythias won a race, Damon was the first person at the finish line to congratulate him. Even as adults, Damon and Pythias remained close and were rarely seen apart.

One day, they visited the city of Syracuse on the island of Sicily. The city's ruler was named King Dionysius, a cruel and quick-tempered king who did not like anyone disagreeing with him. When Damon and Pythias arrived, a large crowd had gathered to hear King Dionysius speak.

"I have written a new law," King Dionysius roared. "All fruit sellers must give part of their profit to the king. The money will be used to build a bigger castle."

The crowd rumbled its disapproval. They did not like the new law. King Dionysius's face turned red with rage as people murmured in protest.

"I don't agree with the law either," Pythias said to Damon. "It is unfair."

Unfortunately, King Dionysius had excellent hearing. He heard Pythias's comment. The king wheeled around and pointed his long finger at Pythias.

"Arrest that man!" King Dionysius yelled. "Bind his hands and take him to the castle!"

The king's soldiers pushed their way through the crowd and grabbed Pythias. They quickly hustled Pythias away and bound his hands. Damon followed his friend all the way to the throne room.

Once there, King Dionysius glared at Pythias. "No one is allowed to criticize my rule. The punishment is death."

Pythias stood proudly in the center of the throne room.

"I disagree with your law," Pythias said. "However, I respect your right as king to make laws. I will not argue with your ruling. Before my punishment, will you allow me to go home and say goodbye to my family? They will be heartbroken if I do not return."

King Dionysius laughed. "You must think that I am a fool," he sneered. "If I let you go, I will never see you again. Surely you will never come back to face your punishment."

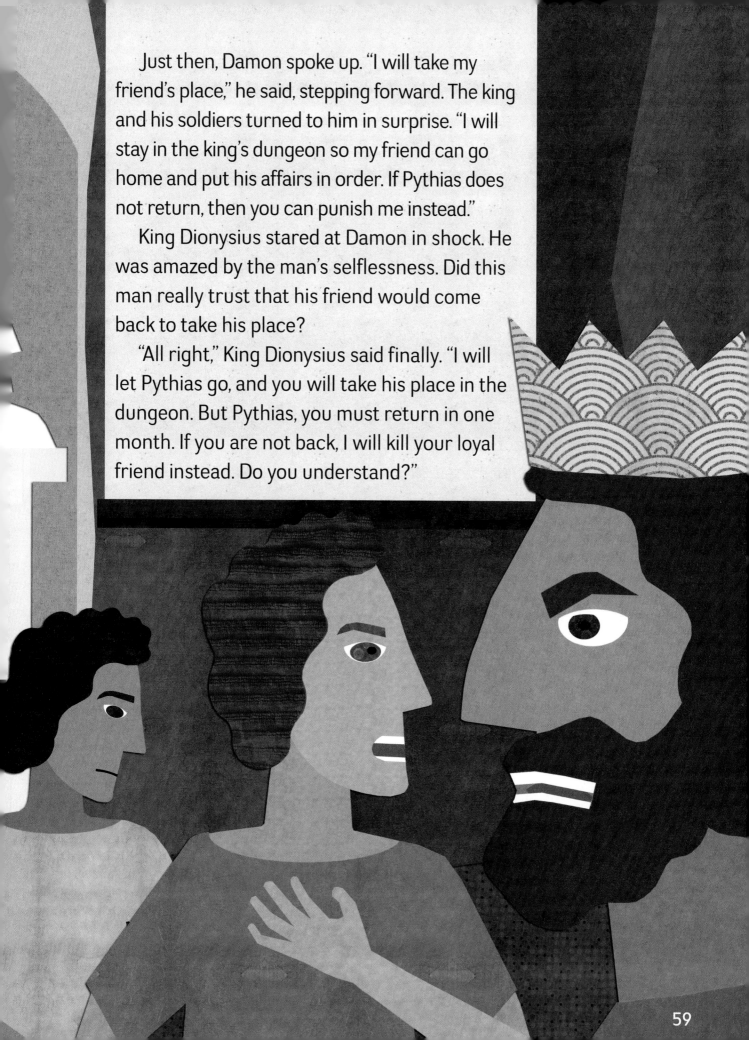

Just then, Damon spoke up. "I will take my friend's place," he said, stepping forward. The king and his soldiers turned to him in surprise. "I will stay in the king's dungeon so my friend can go home and put his affairs in order. If Pythias does not return, then you can punish me instead."

King Dionysius stared at Damon in shock. He was amazed by the man's selflessness. Did this man really trust that his friend would come back to take his place?

"All right," King Dionysius said finally. "I will let Pythias go, and you will take his place in the dungeon. But Pythias, you must return in one month. If you are not back, I will kill your loyal friend instead. Do you understand?"

59

Pythias nodded. The soldiers untied Pythias and used the rope to tie up Damon's hands. The friends shook hands, and Pythias promised he would be back in a month.

Pythias traveled home and said goodbye to his family. They did not want him to return to Syracuse to be killed. But Pythias had made a promise to Damon, and he intended to keep it.

However, on his trip back to Syracuse, Pythias's ship was attacked by pirates. They stole Pythias's money and threw him overboard. Pythias swam to a deserted island and waited for help, but no help came. Pythias was anxious to get back to Damon, so he built a raft out of logs and vines and paddled in the direction of Sicily. He did not know if his plan would work, but he did know he had to try to save Damon.

Back in Syracuse, the weeks passed. As the appointed time drew near, King Dionysius ordered Damon to be brought before him.

"Your friend has abandoned you," the king said, mocking him. "Pythias is not coming. He does not respect you. He has taken advantage of your trust and left you here to die."

"My friend will be here," Damon answered confidently. "He made a promise to me, and I know he will keep that promise."

Finally, the day came for Damon to be put to death. The soldiers marched Damon to the town square where a large crowd had gathered. King Dionysius studied Damon's face.

"You look very calm," the king said. "You are not worried?"

"No," Damon said. "I am confident my friend will come."

King Dionysius laughed at Damon and waved to a soldier. The soldier pulled out his sword and waited for the king's signal. Suddenly, there was a great commotion in the crowd. A dirty, bearded man burst forth and ran to the front. It was Pythias!

"I am here!" he cried. "My ship was seized by pirates. I was thrown overboard, so I swam to a deserted island and built a raft. Once I reached Sicily, I ran all the way to the castle. Thank goodness I am not too late!"

Pythias tried to take Damon's place in front of the king. Damon hugged his friend.

"I knew you would come back," Damon said. The crowd watched with awe.

King Dionysius was so moved by the loyalty between the two friends that he decided to pardon Pythias of the crime. Never before had he seen such respect and friendship as these two showed to each other. He cancelled the death sentence and set both men free. He also vowed to treat his subjects with the same kind of respect he now had for the great friends Damon and Pythias.

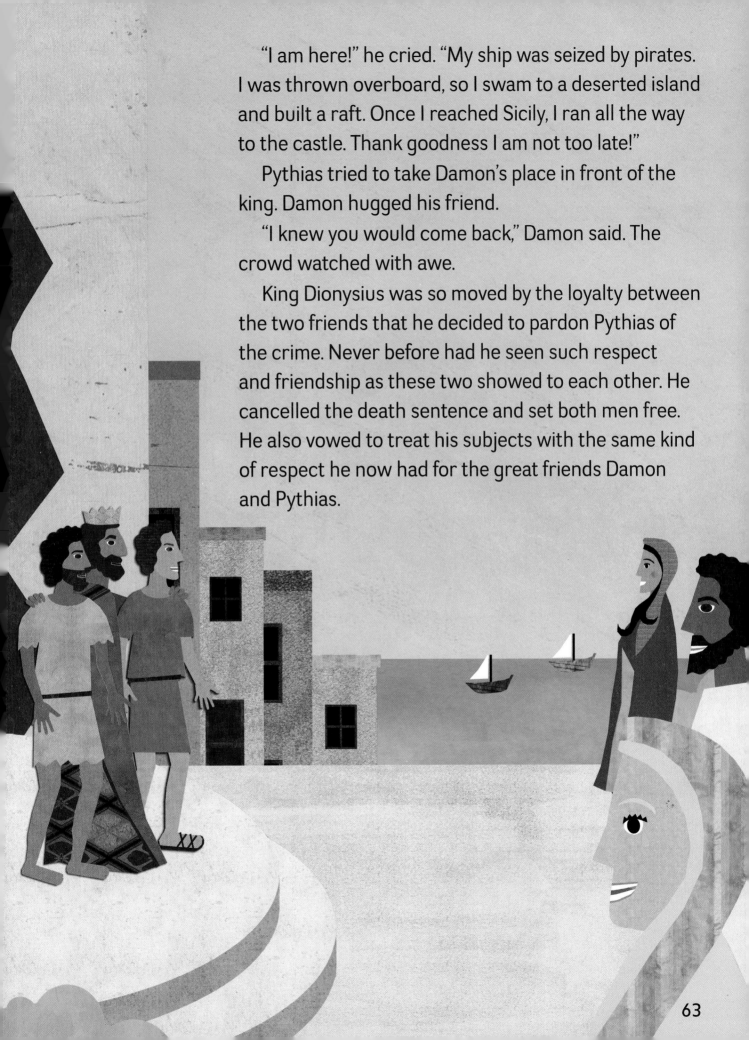

Essential Questions
What does it mean to be responsible?
What are some things you are responsible for?

VOLUNTEERS NEEDED

Duty

by Edwin Markham
illustrated by Tom Herzberg

When Duty comes a-knocking at your gate,
Welcome him in; for if you bid him wait,
He will depart only to come once more
And bring seven other duties to your door.

Jim

by Gwendolyn Brooks
illustrated by Marni Backer

There never was a nicer boy
Than Mrs. Jackson's Jim.
The sun should drop its greatest gold
On him.

Because, when Mother-dear was sick,
He brought her cocoa in.
And brought her broth, and brought
   her bread.
And brought her medicine.

And, tipping, tidied up her room.
And would not let her see
He missed his game of baseball
Terribly.

You will answer the comprehension questions on these pages as a class.

Text Connections

1. What is the evidence that Damon and Pythias are the best of friends? Refer explicitly to the text to support your answer.

2. What is the scariest part of "Damon and Pythias"? Do you think either Damon or Pythias is scared?

3. What do the poems and the story each say about duty and respect?

4. What could Damon and Pythias teach Shima from "The Origami Master" about friendship?

Did You Know?

Syracuse is a historic city in Sicily, Italy. It has a rich, ancient Greek history. Named after this city, Syracuse, New York, is the fifth largest city in the state of New York.

Look Closer

Keys to Comprehension

1. How does King Dionysius get away with his unfair and cruel punishments?

2. Why does King Dionysius change his opinion of Damon and Pythias?

Writer's Craft

3. If you were as powerful as King Dionysius, how would you punish people who disagreed with you?

4. How does each stanza of "Jim" show that Jim cares about his duty?

Concept Development

5. What do the illustrations in the story tell you that the text does not?

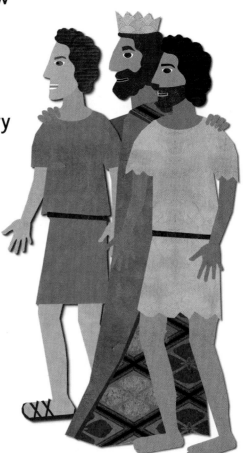

Write

The poems and the story give a lot of examples of duties. Make a list of the duties you have.

Read this article. Then discuss it with your class.

Vocabulary Words

- **anxious**
- **before**
- **criticize**
- **intended**
- **pardon**
- **seized**

Volunteering for the Race

Everybody loves the excitement of a big marathon. Before the start, the anxious runners wait at the starting line. The crowd is on pins and needles. Everybody is holding their breath. Then the buzzer sounds. The runners are off!

It is very exciting, but have you ever wondered who makes the race possible? The New York City marathon can have more than 50,000 runners. And the race can take more than six hours to complete! It takes hundreds of volunteers to ensure that the runners have a safe and fun race.

Many volunteers work at aid stations. They give water and sports drinks to passing runners. Other volunteers try hard to detect if anybody is trying to take a shortcut. Volunteers do not pardon cheaters when they spot them. They may not intend to hurt the other runners, but cheaters are rightfully criticized. They can ruin the race for everybody. It is a hard job, but volunteers have to make sure that all the runners have a level playing field.

Some volunteers hand out medals at the finish line. Running a marathon is never easy. By the time a runner finishes, he or she has spent many hours running and is exhausted. However, when a volunteer places a medal around the runner's neck, he or she knows that the hard work has been worth it.

Runners may get all the attention, but volunteers also deserve our respect. The next time we watch a race, let's remember all the work that happens behind the scenes. When we cheer, let's seize the opportunity. Let's cheer for volunteers, too!

Concept Vocabulary

Think about the word *generous*. What are some things you should be generous with?

Extend Vocabulary

Copy the word web into your Writer's Notebook. Then fill it in with three antonyms and three synonyms for *criticize*.

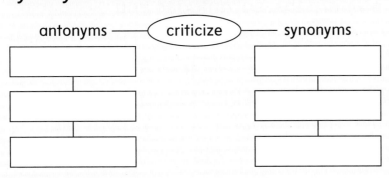

Read this Social Studies Connection. You will answer the questions as a class.

Text Feature

A **map** shows where things are located.

A King's Power

Dionysius I was a real king who ruled southern Italy. He lived from 432–367 BC. He made Syracuse a powerful city. King Dionysius was cruel; people were forced to serve him. He made the people of any city he seized become his slaves. So it is not unusual that he sentenced Pythias to die.

Today there are still countries that have kings or queens. Australia, the Bahamas, Canada, Jamaica, New Zealand, and the United Kingdom are all headed by the King or Queen of England. Each one has its own government as well. Belgium, Denmark, Norway, Spain, and Sweden are other countries in Europe that have kings or queens. Japan has an emperor.

Most of these kings and queens do not have much authority. They are mostly ceremonial, and reminders of the long histories of their countries. Their countries' governments have the real power, and they are elected by the citizens.

Compare the advantages and disadvantages of each form of government: a country ruled by a king or queen and a country ruled by representatives of the people. Think about how they meet the needs of the people who live in the country.

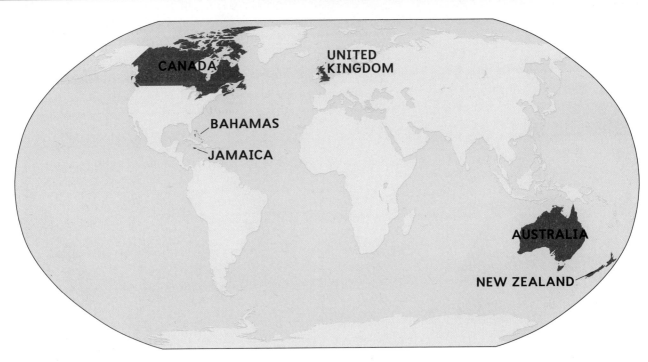

The countries headed by the King or Queen of England

1. Look at the map of the countries headed by the King or Queen of England. Which one is not an island? Which one is a continent? Which one is in Europe?

2. What are some other countries that have a king or queen? Where are these countries located?

3. Do you think Dionysius would last long as king today? Why or why not?

 Go Digital

Search for images of Dionysius I of Syracuse. Then find all the countries that have kings and queens today. Which have the same kind of power that Dionysius had?

Genre Narrative Nonfiction

Essential Questions
Why is it important to stand by your friends?
What is the value of loyalty? How can loyalty
show respect?

Bummer and Lazarus

by Dennis Fertig
illustrated by Josh Brunet

Bummer and Lazarus

In the winter of 1861, a big, black dog dodged moving wagons on a busy San Francisco street. It sniffed here and there as it searched for food. At times, it gently approached humans and looked for dinner. Often someone gave the dog a snack and said, "Here you go, Bummer."

Stray dogs like Bummer were common in San Francisco in the 1860s. These dogs were part of great changes in the city. Before the year 1849, San Francisco had been a tiny village. Then gold was discovered nearby. People rushed to San Francisco. They came by horse and wagon. They came in ships. They all hoped to get rich. Some did. Most did not. But the small village quickly grew into a city of more than 50,000 people.

When people came to find gold, they often brought dogs with them. Over time, many dogs became homeless strays. Soon there were too many stray dogs!

Yet many strays were friendly and likeable. Bummer was one of those. He looked as if he was always smiling. That is one reason that people fed him. But people fed Bummer and other dogs for another reason. These dogs were good at getting rid of another animal pest—rats!

Rats also came to San Francisco on ships. That was a common way for rats to see the world! In their new city, rats had very, very large families.

Many types of dogs have been bred to hunt rats. These dogs work hard to get rid of them. Bummer was an expert rat hunter. He could quickly destroy a nest of dozens of rats. People were happy to have dogs like Bummer around the neighborhood.

Bummer Becomes Famous

Bummer's neighborhood was filled with newspaper offices and reporters. The reporters were always looking for interesting stories.

On a January day in 1861, Bummer did something that made him very interesting. A crowd of people watched a terrible fight between a large, nasty dog and a much smaller one. It looked as if the smaller dog might not survive.

Suddenly, a third dog raced into the battle. It was Bummer! He immediately chased the large dog away. He saved the small dog's life.

Then Bummer did more. He led the wounded dog to a doorway to heal. At night, Bummer would protect the smaller dog from the cold, unfriendly strays. Bummer even shared food he had received from humans with the poor dog. In fact, Bummer made sure that the small dog ate before he did.

Newspaper reporters wrote about Bummer's unselfish acts. The reporters even gave the small dog a name—Lazarus. As Lazarus healed, he made the rounds with Bummer. The people of San Francisco treated Bummer as a hero.

After Lazarus was healthy, he and Bummer stayed great pals. It turned out that Lazarus was also good at hunting rats. The famous duo of Bummer and Lazarus quickly grew in popularity.

More Stories

Over the next few years, there were many stories about Bummer and Lazarus. The best stories described Bummer and Lazarus's clever adventures. For example, stories explained how the pair worked together to get bones away from other dogs. People were delighted that Bummer and Lazarus were working as a team.

One story was hard to believe. When a runaway horse raced down a busy street, Bummer and Lazarus ran alongside it until Bummer could cut in front of it. That slowed the horse down so a man could grab its reins. Were Bummer and Lazarus that smart?

The dogs did misbehave now and then. More than once, the dogs were locked in a store overnight. They were supposed to get rid of rats, but instead they destroyed much of the store trying to get out. Bummer and Lazarus loved their freedom.

Once, Bummer was injured and unable to get his own food. People worried about him. During this time, Lazarus brought Bummer food, but only after he had eaten some himself. The people of San Francisco loved Lazarus, but knew that no dog was as caring as Bummer.

Special Treatment

As the adventures of Bummer and Lazarus continued, the city's love for the pair grew too. Crowds welcomed them wherever they went. Someone took Lazarus to the dog pound once. People across the city demanded he be set free. After that, the friends were free to roam the town without fear of the dog catcher.

During this time, Bummer and Lazarus continued to rid the city of rats. And they continued to enjoy the love, respect, and food of many San Francisco citizens. Their adventures filled the papers.

Tragedy Strikes

Stray dogs in San Francisco still faced risks every day though, even famous ones. One October morning in 1863, Lazarus ate something he should not have. The poor dog died. When newspapers reported the story, sadness spread over the city.

Of course nobody, human or dog, was as sad as Bummer. For the rest of his life, Bummer never wandered too far from where he last saw Lazarus. That made people love Bummer even more.

Eventually, brave Bummer was seriously injured on a city street. The newspapers gave daily reports about his health. People hoped Bummer would get better, but he did not. When Bummer died in the fall of 1865, sadness again filled the city.

Two Dogs Remembered

After Bummer and Lazarus were gone, more stories about them were told. As years passed, people wondered if Bummer and Lazarus could have been real. They were!

They were great friends who looked out for each other and for the city of San Francisco. They even became known as "the Damon and Pythias of dogs" in honor of the legendary friends from ancient Greece.

In 1992, the city put up a plaque to honor the two dogs. It ends with these words:

Two dogs, but with a single bark,
Two tails that wagged as one.

The city of San Francisco still loves Bummer and Lazarus.

The Clownfish to the Anemone

by Ann Harland

I need you to protect me—
your stinging tentacles, you see,
scare off predators who'd eat me.

You need me for protection, too.
I swim and dart, guarding you,
keeping fierce fish from harming you.

We work together, we agree.
You don't sting me, and I let you be.
We care for each other in the deep,
dark sea.

You will answer the comprehension questions on these pages as a class.

Text Connections

1. How did Bummer and Lazarus meet? Find the place in the text that describes their first encounter.

2. Why did newspaper reporters write stories about Bummer and Lazarus?

3. What message does "The Clownfish to the Anemone" share with "Bummer and Lazarus"?

4. Which is the stronger relationship: Bummer and Lazarus or Damon and Pythias? Explain your answer.

Did You Know?

Lazarus was named after a religious figure that was sick and died, then was brought back to life. Before Bummer nursed him back to health, Lazarus was not expected to live, so Lazarus is a good name for him.

Look Closer

Keys to Comprehension

1. What advantages did Bummer and Lazarus have over other dogs because they were liked by people?

Writer's Craft

2. How do the section titles in "Bummer and Lazarus" help organize the information and make it easier to find?

3. Who is the speaker in the poem? How do you know?

Concept Development

4. What happened after Lazarus died?

5. Why were Bummer and Lazarus called "the Damon and Pythias" of dogs?

Write

Write about a time you made a sacrifice for a friend, or a friend made a sacrifice for you. How did it make you feel?

Read this story. Then discuss it with your class.

Vocabulary Words

- **cold**
- **common**
- **heal**
- **reins**
- **spread**
- **unselfish**

Farm Memories

Every morning, Sara and her father walked around the farm to check on the animals. One morning, they saw that one of the horses was missing. Sara gasped. She pointed to a hole in their fence that was spread out before them. The horse had escaped! "Stay here," her father said. "Capturing him could be dangerous. He might kick when I put on his reins." Sara wanted to come, but she knew that her father was right. She stayed behind.

While checking on the other animals, Sara spied a deer caught in the fence. One of its legs was twisted in the wire. It was common for deer to become trapped this way.

Sara tried to untwist the wire, but she was not strong enough. She grabbed a fallen branch and tried to pry out the deer's leg. The wires barely moved. The deer struggled to free itself. *Calm down, girl*, Sara thought. *I'm here to help.*

Sara twisted the branch as hard as she could. Little by little, she began to loosen the wires. Finally, the deer jerked its leg from the fence and ran off into the forest.

"I'm sorry," her father said when he came back, leading the escaped horse. "I did not mean to sound cold when I told you not to come. I saw you help the deer. That was very unselfish."

At the edge of the forest, Sara saw the deer drinking from a small stream. It looked hurt, but it would heal soon. "It's okay," she told her father. "I know you were worried about me. I am happy to help however I can."

Concept Vocabulary

Think about the word *devotion*. What are some things you have a devotion to?

Extend Vocabulary

Answer and explain the following questions.

- When Sara's father put *reins* on the horse, was he trying to control it or set it free?
- If the deer will *heal* soon, will it get bigger soon or get healthy soon?
- If deer are *common*, does Sara see them frequently or very rarely?

Read this Science Connection. You will answer the questions as a class.

Text Feature

A **Venn diagram** is a graphic organizer that is useful for comparing and contrasting.

City Habitats

People do not usually think of cities, like San Francisco in "Bummer and Lazarus," as animal habitats, but they are. Some living things cannot survive in a city. Some survive poorly, and some thrive.

An elephant would not be able to find the food, water, shelter, and climate that it needs to survive in a city, unless it was in a zoo. Bummer and Lazarus got help to survive. People fed them and watched out for them. However, some animals, like the rats Bummer and Lazarus hunted, find just what they need in a city habitat.

Rats live wherever humans can be found. They are active at night when people are sleeping. They like living in sewers where nobody bothers them. They also spread into alleyways and buildings.

Being omnivores, rats eat whatever is available to them. Garbage is a tasty treat. They will dig and chew through all kinds of materials to get to food. Rats find that human cities meet their needs quite nicely.

Think of other animals that are common in city habitats. What allows each animal to survive in cities? How are they similar to rats? How are they different?

City Dwellers

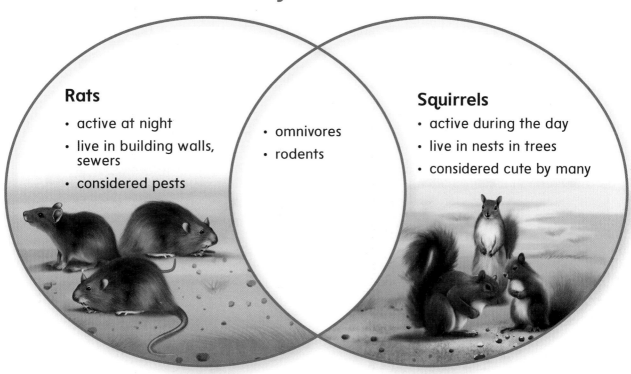

Rats
- active at night
- live in building walls, sewers
- considered pests

- omnivores
- rodents

Squirrels
- active during the day
- live in nests in trees
- considered cute by many

1. What animals live in cities? How have they adapted to a city habitat?

2. What animals could not survive in a city? What do they need that a city habitat does not provide?

3. What does each section of the Venn diagram show? What are some other entries you can add to the diagram?

 Go Digital

Search for information about how rats survive in cities. Then look for other animals that call cities their homes.

The Prairie Fire

by Marilynn Reynolds
illustrated by Don Kilby

Genre Historical Fiction

Essential Questions

What kinds of people show bravery in the face of danger? Why do we admire people like firefighters and astronauts?

There was a time when terrible fires swept
for miles across the prairie. The fires started in
spring and fall, when the land was dry, and they
burned the grasses, the trees, the sod houses, and
everything in their path.

"Watch for a cloud of smoke in the sky," Father
told Percy one fall afternoon. "If a prairie fire's
coming, that's the first thing you'll see. And if a
high wind's blowing, that fire will race across the
prairie faster than wild horses."

Mother reached over and took Percy's hand. "Maybe there won't be any fires this year," she said. But her eyes looked worried. It was already the beginning of October, and the grass around the homestead was as parched as straw.

"Tomorrow I'll start to plow a fireguard around the house and barn," Father said wearily. "If a prairie fire comes this way, there'll be no grass for it to burn and it'll pass us by."

Percy looked at Father's heavy shoulders, his sunburned neck, and his big scarred fingers. "I can plow too," he said.

But Father shook his head. "You can help me when you're bigger."

That night Percy dreamed about the fire running with the wind. Running as fast as a galloping horse. Racing straight toward their house with nothing to stop it.

Early next morning Father got up in the dark and went out to the barn to hitch the oxen—Old Jim and Frank—to the plow. All week Percy watched as his father and the oxen plowed a giant circle around the house, the barn, and the haystacks. Every day the circle of plowed land grew wider.

"The fireguard's almost twenty yards across," Father said with satisfaction at supper one night. "If a fire heads this way, there'll be hardly a blade of grass to burn around the homestead." He smiled. "I'll plow one last round tomorrow, then I think we'll be safe."

"I'm big enough," Percy said the next day. "Can't I help Dad plow the last part of the fireguard?"

His mother shook her head. "Maybe another year, when you're older." She smiled at his sad face. "Why don't you go out and feed Maud?"

Percy slowly trudged across the yard to the barn. Maud's white coat gleamed in the dark. He breathed in the sweet smell of the mare's sweat and stroked her neck. "Dad thinks I'm too little to help," he said. Maud chewed the hay with her big teeth and whinnied softly.

When Maud finished, Percy left the barn and ran across the fireguard and out onto the prairie. All around him, the land stretched brown in the October sunshine. It was strangely empty. The crows, blackbirds, and robins had flown south, and the gophers were deep in their holes underground. Silence lay everywhere.

A cold, brisk breeze stirred the grass. Percy heard a noise like a pack of barking dogs. He looked up. Overhead, in a long wavy vee, a flock of late-migrating geese was traveling to warmer lands. Percy's heart soared with the birds as they grew smaller and farther away.

And that's when he saw it. A bluish-black cloud to the southeast.

Even as Percy watched, the cloud grew larger and larger. Suddenly he realized that it wasn't an ordinary cloud.

It was smoke – smoke from a prairie fire.

Somewhere, miles away, lightning had lit the grasses. Or a settler's campfire had escaped. Now a prairie fire was running across the land with a high wind at its back, burning everything in its path.

Percy sank to his knees and stared at the black cloud. He couldn't move. He felt frozen to the grass.

Then Percy sprang to his feet. He raced back to the fireguard. "Dad!" he shouted as he ran. "Smoke! I see smoke!"

Percy's father got off the plow and squinted at the horizon. "Help me unyoke the oxen," he said quietly.

As Percy and his father worked, Old Jim and Frank began to move about uneasily. Old Jim sniffed the air and tossed his head from side to side. Frank pawed the ground.

"They smell the smoke," his father said.

When the oxen were free, Father whacked them on the rump. "Save yourselves, boys!" he shouted, as the pair stumbled off across the prairie toward the water in the slough.

Leaving the plow where it stood, Father and Percy ran back to the homestead. "Fire!" they shouted as Mother rushed out of the house. "A fire's coming!"

The smell of smoke was stronger now. When Percy and his father reached the barn, they found Maud bolting around in her stall. Father tried to quiet the mare as he led her out into the yard. She danced nervously while he hitched her to the flat stoneboat. Quickly he led the horse to the rain barrel beside the house. Father heaved the barrel, heavy with rainwater, onto the stoneboat and thrust an empty pail into Percy's hands.

"You and Maud will have to guard the haystacks and the buildings," Father said. "If sparks land here, douse them with water. Mother and I'll go to the fireguard and put out any sparks that land there."

"Don't go!" Percy cried, hanging onto his father's arm. Percy hung his head. "I'm afraid of the fire," he whispered.

His father hugged Percy tight to his chest. And his mother kissed him. But there was no time to waste. Gathering up all the gunnysacks they could find, his parents ran out to the fireguard. Percy and the horse were left alone in the yard.

Percy's nose and eyes stung from the smoke as the fire came closer. Within minutes the hissing and crackling flames reached the homestead. Showers of sparks sailed over the fireguard and dropped into the barnyard.

"Come on, Maud!" In the flickering red light of the fire, Percy pulled Maud over to the sparks. Sometimes the smoke was so thick and the air so hot that he could scarcely breathe. But he led Maud around the yard, pulling the rain barrel to places where the sparks landed and dousing them with his pail of water.

Then, to Percy's amazement, two rabbits and a coyote ran into the yard to escape the flames. When the terrified animals ran past Percy's feet, Maud started. She began to kick, and the precious barrel of rainwater rocked back and forth on the stoneboat. Maud screamed, and for the first time in his life, Percy was afraid of her. He tried to calm the mare, but Maud reared high above him. Water sloshed out of the rain barrel, and the horse's reins swung out of Percy's reach.

"Dad! Dad, help me!" he shouted. Through the smoke he could see his parents against the orange sky, beating out the sparks. He could hear them shouting to each other. But in the noise of the fire they couldn't hear him.

Again and again Percy jumped up to grab Maud's reins. But Maud kept twisting her head away. At last Percy ran to the barn. He came back with his arms full of hay and laid it before the rearing horse.

At the sight of the hay, Maud quieted. She bent her head and took a mouthful. With trembling fingers, Percy undid the buttons of his old cotton shirt and pulled it off his shoulders. As the mare ate, he tied the shirt across her eyes like a bandage.

Percy grabbed the reins and pulled the blindfolded horse toward the small fires that had started up in the farmyard. At first Maud whinnied and pulled back, but finally she shuddered and followed him.

Back and forth they went, from the haystacks to the barn and to the sod house. Back and forth until there were fewer and fewer fires to put out.

At last there were none. With a rush of hot air, the prairie fire passed by the homestead.

Percy's mother and father came through the smoke and staggered, coughing, into the farmyard. Their eyes were red and their faces and clothes black with charred grass and soot. When they saw Percy through the haze, they ran to him, and the family clung together in the smoking yard.

Late that afternoon, Percy and his parents stood in the doorway of the sod house. Curls of smoke drifted up around the haystacks and little fires still smoldered along the fireguard. Out on the prairie, the path of the fire was charred black to the edge of the sky.

"Do you think Old Jim and Frank are all right?" Percy asked, anxiously.

Father put his arm around Percy's shoulders. "They had plenty of time to reach the slough, and they probably waded out into the water where the fire couldn't reach them. Those boys are a pretty smart pair. They must be hungry by now. I think I'll walk down to the slough and drive them back to the barn."

Father looked down at Percy and smiled. "It's a job for two men. Why don't you come with me, Son? I'll need your help."

Text Connections

1. Why is Percy not allowed to help his father plow? Why does Percy's father let him help fight the fire?

2. How does Percy help fight the fire?

3. How does Percy earn his parents' respect? Use evidence from the text to support your answer.

4. What other characters in the stories from this unit have earned respect?

Did You Know?

An ox is similar to a cow and is trained to pull carts, wagons, or plows. Before the invention of machines like trucks and tractors, these animals were common to farms and usually worked in pairs.

Look Closer

Keys to Comprehension

1. What are the conditions that make the prairie fire possible?

2. How does Father's impression of Percy change over the course of the story?

Writer's Craft

3. The grass around Percy's homestead is described as being "as parched as straw." What does that phrase mean?

4. How does Percy show his fear? What would you have done if you were in Percy's situation?

Concept Development

5. How do the illustrations in the story help you understand key details about the setting?

Write

Write a guide for how you can equip yourself and your home to stay safe from a fire. Include illustrations to help your reader visualize what they will need.

Read this article. Then discuss it with your class.

Vocabulary Words

- **douse**
- **drive**
- **guard**
- **heart**
- **homestead**
- **pack**
- **parched**
- **sod**
- **thrust**
- **trudged**
- **waste**
- **yards**

Fire Safety

What should you do if there is a fire in your home? Here are some helpful tips to guard against a dangerous fire:

- Take fire safety to heart. A fire can break out anywhere. It may come when you are not expecting it.
- Inside, make sure you have smoke detectors. Check the batteries twice a year. Look around for safety hazards, too. You could have a bad outlet or cord.
- Outside, never leave coals or wood burning. If you have a bonfire or cookout, make sure you douse it before you walk away. Parched sod, sticks, or leaves can burn quickly.
- If you live on a homestead, learn how to build a fireguard to protect your land and animal pack. A fireguard is a section of ground with nothing that will burn. All grass and plants must be removed. Only dirt should remain. When a fire reaches a fireguard, it stops and cannot go any farther.
- Build an emergency kit. Put in a flashlight and a fire extinguisher. If your home has more than one floor, a fire may drive you upstairs.

A rope ladder at least several yards long could help you escape. Put it in a handy place so you can thrust it through an open window if you are trapped by a fire.

- Do not panic. By remaining calm, you can think and act properly. You should not trudge through your house in a fire, but acting too quickly and without thought can be just as dangerous.
- Make a fire escape plan. Know where to go in an emergency. Think about where to go to get help. Everyone should know what to do so they do not panic or waste time.

Staying safe from fire requires a good plan, a calm head, and most importantly, a dedication to preventing a fire in the first place.

Concept Vocabulary

Think about the word *courage*. When did you or somebody you know have to show courage?

Extend Vocabulary

Copy the word web into your Writer's Notebook. Fill it in with words related to trudged. That could include antonyms, synonyms, or related words.

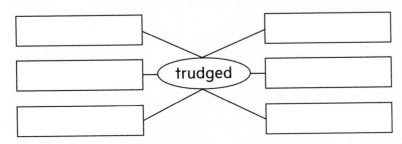

Read this Social Studies Connection. You will answer the questions as a class.

Text Feature

A **list** is a way of organizing information.

Civic Ideals

After reading "The Prairie Fire," you know how dangerous a fire could be to homesteads in the 1800s. Families had to guard against and fight fires by themselves. There were no fire departments out in rural areas. Things are different today, even in places with few people.

When a fire breaks out today, people can reach out for help. Many rural areas have a volunteer fire department. People from the community come together and race to douse the flames. Helping those in need is a sign of respect. It is also a civic ideal. Civic ideals and practices are the unselfish things people do for the common good and to build a community.

Examples of civic ideals include being fair, supporting the common good, following the rules, and taking the responsibility to better your community. You can practice living up to civic ideals right in your classroom:

1. First, create a list of civic ideals for your classroom.

2. Then, describe how the ideals benefit the common good.

3. Finally, put them to practice.

1. What are some of the civic ideals you read about? How can you live up to those ideals?

2. How is the volunteer firefighter in the photo above living up to civic ideals? Who else in your community practices civic ideals?

3. What is the difference between the numbered list on page 112 and the bulleted list on pages 110–111?

 Go Digital

Search for examples of acts of kindness or generosity that followed a natural disaster. Find stories about people who practice civic ideals.

Genre Play

Essential Questions
What makes somebody a good person?
How do actions speak louder than words?

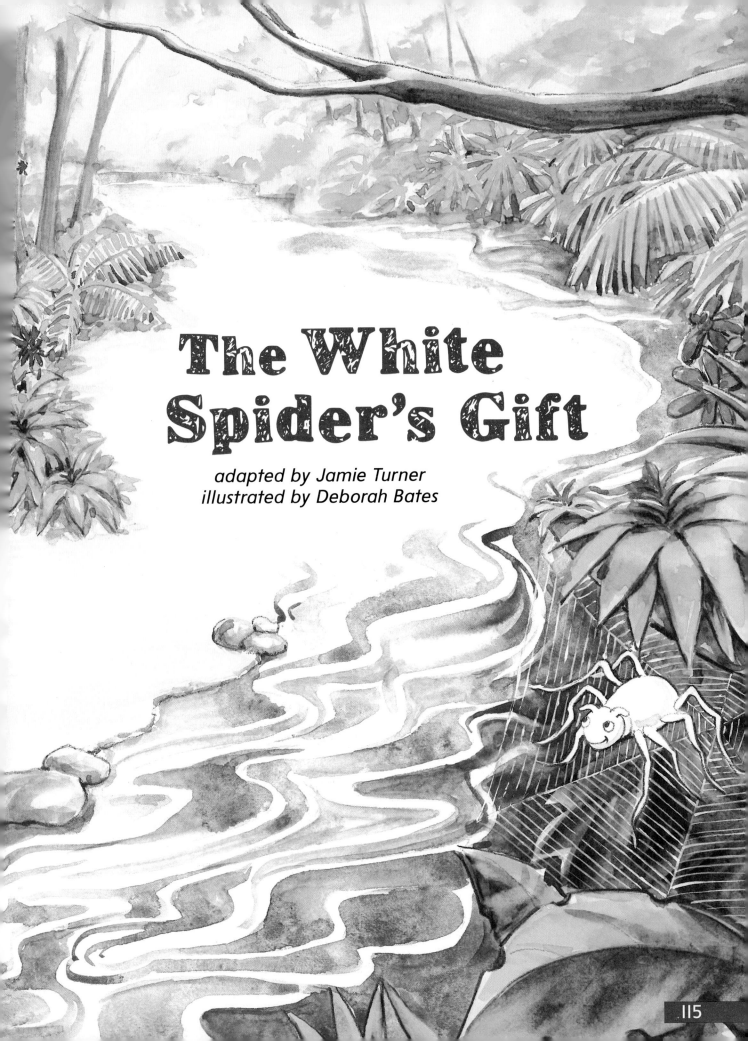

The White Spider's Gift

adapted by Jamie Turner
illustrated by Deborah Bates

Characters

WHITE SPIDER, offstage voice

KUMA, Guarani boy

TWO GIRLS

OLD WOMAN

PIKI, Guarani boy

MOTHER, Piki's mother

TUKIRA, Chieftain's daughter

THREE WOMEN

CHIEFTAIN

MESSENGER

DIKA

DABU

KINTA

MUNGA

— Guarani boys

SCENE 1

TIME: *Long ago.*

SETTING: *Forest of Paraguay. Played before curtain. Murals on walls flanking stage depict trees and undergrowth. One large bush, displayed on right wall outside curtain, represents spider's home. Bush must be visible throughout the play. A large spider's web of white yarn covers most of the bush.*

BEFORE RISE: *KUMA enters left, and runs toward spider's web.*

SPIDER *(From offstage):* Help me! Please, I am over here in the spring!

KUMA *(Stopping; irritably):* What? Who are you? *(Peers over stage apron)*

SPIDER: Please, will you bend down here and lift me out? I have fallen into the spring.

KUMA: What? Help a spider? I cannot stop for such a small matter. I must go find tea leaves for my father. I have already wasted much time, and he will be angry.

SPIDER *(Pleading):* Oh, please. I would not trouble you if I were not so tired. The water bubbles up so, and I cannot reach the edge.

KUMA *(Looking up at sky):* I must hurry. Father is waiting. *(Runs out. 1ST GIRL enters at side, looks along floor as if hunting.)*

SPIDER: Please, little girl, help me! See, I am here in the spring.

1ST GIRL *(Stooping):* Where? Oh, I see—why, you are a spider! I am afraid of spiders! And you are a white one, besides; I have never seen a white spider. You must be ill. I cannot help you; I might get hurt.

SPIDER: I am harmless, little girl. Please help me. My strength is almost gone.

1ST GIRL: Oh, but I could not bear to touch a spider. Swim to the edge and climb out yourself. Spiders are good climbers.

SPIDER: I cannot! The water swirls around me with great force; it is stronger than I am.

1ST GIRL: If I remember, I will send a friend to help you when I get back to the village. I am looking for the beautiful nandari flower now. I cannot stop. *(Exits, humming and stooping to examine flowers. OLD WOMAN with walking stick enters, shuffles toward spider web, dragging burlap sack behind her.)*

SPIDER *(Calling):* Kind woman! Please help me!
(OLD WOMAN cocks head, puts hand to ear)

OLD WOMAN: What is it that I hear?

SPIDER: It is I, the little white spider who lives in the yerba bush beside the spring.

OLD WOMAN *(Looking up at web):* Eh? Who? Where?

SPIDER: No, not up there. I am down here in the water! I fell from my web and cannot get out. Please help me!

OLD WOMAN *(Looking over edge of stage; shaking head, sadly):* Ah, yes, life is full of trouble, little spider. And the older one gets, the more burdened with care he becomes.

SPIDER: But will you not help me, Guarani woman? Will you not hold your stick down and let me crawl upon it so that you may lift me out?

OLD WOMAN: I am old, little spider. I must help myself. I must look for twigs so that I may have a fire tonight. *(Exits, mumbling)* Trouble, trouble. Life is full of trouble. *(PIKI and MOTHER enter, carrying large earthen jars, and walk across stage.)*

SPIDER: Help! Oh, please! I am growing weak! Please help me!

PIKI: Do you hear a cry for help?

MOTHER: Yes, Piki, I do. *(Calls)* Where are you?

SPIDER: Here in the spring! *(Voice grows fainter.)* I cannot swim any longer. My legs are...

PIKI (Dropping to knees and looking over edge of stage): Oh, Mother, it is a spider. She is sinking! *(Reaches down. "Spider" may be concealed in PIKI's hand when he first enters or hidden on ledge near spring.)*

MOTHER: Can you reach her, Piki?

PIKI *(Rising, cupping hand gently):* Yes. Oh, I hope she's still alive!

MOTHER: Oh, Piki, see—she opens her eyes!

PIKI *(Patting inside hand with finger):* Little spider, are you really alive? I am so happy I could catch you before the water pulled you down.

MOTHER: Is this the little white spider who lives in the yerba bush there beside the spring? *(Looks up at web)*

PIKI: Yes. I see her each day when I come to fill the water jars. She lives so quietly and peacefully, spinning her beautiful web of silk. I am pleased that I could help her.

SPIDER *(Weakly):* Thank you, kind Piki. You are a good, strong young Guarani.

PIKI: Strong? But it does not take strength to lift a small spider.

SPIDER: No, it does not take a strong body, Piki, but it takes a strong heart. A selfless heart is the strongest of all. I am feeling better now. Will you please place me back in my web so that I may rest?

PIKI: Certainly. *(Places SPIDER in center of web)* Rest quietly, little friend. I will visit you tomorrow to see if you are well. Goodbye.

SPIDER: Goodbye, Piki. Someday I shall help you as you have helped me this day. *(PIKI stoops as if filling jar with water. MOTHER takes it from him and gives him another to fill. TUKIRA enters at side, pretending to gather berries, placing them into basket. PIKI looks up and sees her; he stands slowly, gazing in wonder. TUKIRA sees him, looks down quickly, turns and runs off.)*

PIKI: Mother! Who is she?

MOTHER: She is Tukira, the chieftain's daughter.

PIKI: But why have I never seen her before?

MOTHER: When Tukira was a small child, her mother died, and the chieftain sent her to live with an aunt in a distant village. She is sixteen now and has come back to our village to live. The chieftain will soon choose a husband for her.

PIKI: How will he do that?

MOTHER: Tomorrow he will assemble the young men from our village and announce his plan. You will be among them.

PIKI *(Lifting jar to his shoulder):* Tukira...what a beautiful name.

MOTHER *(Lifting other jar):* Yes. A beautiful name for a beautiful princess. Let us start home now, Piki. It is growing late. *(They exit. Curtain)*

126

SCENE 2

TIME: *The next day.*

SETTING: *Chieftain's home. Cloth-covered wooden frame center has leafy branches laid across the top. Large earthen jars, weaving frame, and wood for fire are on either side. Background mural shows forest.*

AT RISE: *CHIEFTAIN sits on floor beneath frame. 1ST WOMAN pretends to cook over open fire. 2ND WOMAN, carrying earthen jar, crosses stage and exits. CHILDREN run across, laughing as they play tag. 3RD WOMAN pretends to weave on loom. MESSENGER enters and bows before CHIEFTAIN.*

CHIEFTAIN: Have the six youths received my message to come today?

MESSENGER *(Bowing):* Yes, Chieftain. They come now. *(PIKI, DIKA, DABU, KINTA, MUNGA, and KUMA enter, carrying bows and arrows. All but CHIEFTAIN, MESSENGER, and boys exit. Boys stand on either side of CHIEFTAIN, with backs to audience.)*

CHIEFTAIN: You all ran well, but you, Kuma, finished first. (*PIKI drops his head briefly but raises it again.*) Next is the shooting contest. (*Points off left*) Do you see the red feather on the trunk of the old tree beside the river? (*Boys nod.*) The one whose arrow pierces the tip of the feather will win this contest. (*MESSENGER stands far left, announcing results of each boy's shot.*) Munga, you may try first. (*One at a time boys stand, facing left, and raise their bows slowly as if to aim an arrow.*)

MUNGA (*Shooting*)*:* How close is it?

MESSENGER: It is very close, only a hand's length from the feather's tip. (*MUNGA runs out left. KINTA shoots next and runs out left.*) That was a good shot, but the first arrow is still closer.

DABU: Surely I can shoot closer. I will pretend the feather is the forehead of a wild boar. (*Shoots, exits*)

MESSENGER: Dabu's arrow is only a finger's width from the tip of the feather! *(DABU shouts joyfully.)*

DIKA: Save your joy, Dabu. There are three more of us to try. *(Shoots)*

MESSENGER: Your arrow did not fly true, Dika. It fell far beneath the feather. *(DIKA exits, disappointed.)*

KUMA *(Boastfully):* With my new bow I can easily win. Watch how straight my arrow will fly! *(Shoots)* I won, did I not?

MESSENGER: No, Kuma, your arrow has fallen near the bottom of the feather's stem, not its tip. Now, Piki, it is your turn. *(KUMA stalks angrily right and sits, sulking.)*

KUMA: You will never win, Piki. You are the youngest of us. Have you ever even held a bow before?

PIKI: I have held a bow for many years, Kuma. This was my father's bow, and it has never failed me. *(Shoots. Boys and MESSENGER shout excitedly and run back onstage, with MESSENGER holding feather aloft. Feather is large and may be made out of red construction paper, cut partway down the middle as if split by the arrow.)*

MESSENGER: See, Piki, your arrow pierced the feather's tip, dividing it exactly in half. You have won! *(KUMA scowls angrily.)*

CHIEFTAIN: Kuma has won the foot race, and Piki has won the shooting contest. Now you will all wrestle. *(MESSENGER hands CHIEFTAIN a stick.)* You will hold this stick between you, and you must keep both hands on the stick at all times. You may not move your feet once the contest begins. The one who can force the other to lose his balance will win. Kuma and Dika will fight first. *(KUMA and DIKA face each other with stick between them, each grasping it with both hands. They plant their feet firmly.)*

MESSENGER: Begin. *(KUMA and DIKA begin their "fight." After brief struggle, DIKA loses balance, and KUMA wins. Next, DABU and KINTA fight, and DABU wins. Then MUNGA and PIKI fight, and PIKI wins.)*

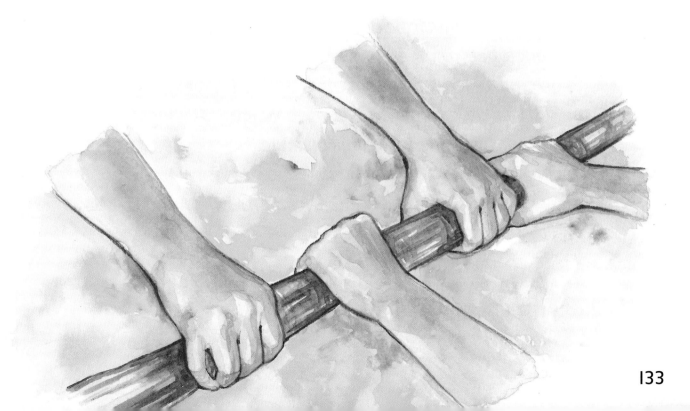

CHIEFTAIN: Now the three winners will fight. First, Piki and Dabu. *(PIKI and DABU face each other and begin. Others form semicircle behind them, upstage, facing audience, but KUMA stands in back of others, drops to ground, takes tube out of his waistband, and aims at PIKI's ankle, as if blowing stone or dart. PIKI winces and grabs his ankle, losing his balance. No one else appears to see what KUMA did.)* Dabu has won. Now, Dabu, you and Kuma will fight. *(DABU and KUMA fight, and DABU wins after a struggle.)*

KUMA *(Throwing stick down angrily)*: It was not fair! I was not ready to start!

CHIEFTAIN: Dabu is the winner. *(Looks around at boys)* You have all done well today, but only three have won. Kuma, Piki, and Dabu will now compete in another contest, which will end in three days. The winner will marry my daughter Tukira on that day. *(DIKA, KINTA, and MUNGA exit; CHIEFTAIN addresses remaining three.)* Each of you must find a beautiful gift to present to my daughter. Return in three days with your gifts, and she will choose the best. Go now and may your search be rewarded. *(Drum beats as KUMA, DABU, and PIKI exit. Curtain)*

SCENE 3

TIME: *Two days later.*

SETTING: *The forest; before curtain.*

BEFORE RISE: *PIKI enters, carrying jar. He approaches spring, kneels down as if to fill jar, then sets jar beside him and sits, looking sad.*

SPIDER *(From offstage):* Piki, Piki, why do you look so sad?

PIKI *(Looking up at bush in surprise):* Oh, it is you, little spider. *(Sighs)* My heart is heavy because I shall not win the beautiful Tukira for my wife. I ran well, I shot well, and I fought well. But now I have no hope. Tukira will surely become the wife of Kuma or Dabu.

SPIDER: You can win the final contest with my help.

PIKI: Do you know of the contest?

SPIDER: Yes. I listen as I sit quietly in my yerba bush spinning my web. The women talk as they come to fill their water jars. I heard them speak of the gifts for the lovely princess.

PIKI: Yes, the lovely princess...but she will never be mine. Tomorrow we must present our gifts. It is said that Dabu will bring a headdress woven of colorful feathers from rare birds. And Kuma boasts openly of his gift, a necklace of gold, encrusted with the lovely topaz stones of the highlands. But I...I have nothing. My mother and I are poor, unlike the families of Dabu and Kuma.

SPIDER: Piki, did you not hear me? I shall help you win Tukira's hand.

PIKI: But how can you help, little spider?

SPIDER: Go home to your mother, Piki, but return to the spring at sunrise. Your special gift for Tukira will be ready. Be joyful, Piki, for the morning will dawn bright.

PIKI *(Puzzled yet hopeful):* I shall do as you say, little friend. Bless you for giving me hope.

SPIDER: Bless you, Piki, for taking time to save me from the bubbling spring. I promised on that day to repay your kindness, and I will. *(PIKI exits, looking back in wonder at spider's bush. Lights dim and music plays softly, indicating nighttime.)* I will spin my most delicate thread and sprinkle it with moon dust. In the center I will form the beautiful guava flower... the loveliest I have ever spun.

And then, rare orchids of many designs. Then I shall spin stars to twinkle around the edges, and then I shall weave all the designs together with a fine, intricate lace. Now I will begin my work, for I must finish before the sun reaches the horizon. *(Music continues for 30 seconds, with lights gradually coming up. Music stops.)*

PIKI *(Entering left, approaching bush):* The new day has dawned, and I have returned as you said, friend.

SPIDER: Look beneath the bush, Piki. I have finished your gift.

PIKI *(Removing lace mantle from bush; holding it up):* Oh, it is beautiful! Never have I seen such delicate lace! It is fit for a princess.

SPIDER: It will be Tukira's bridal veil. Now, hurry home to show it to your mother, and then take it to the chieftain at the appointed time.

PIKI: How I thank you, White Spider! *(Gently folds lace and turns to exit, but KUMA enters, blocks his way. PIKI hides lace behind his back.)*

KUMA: Piki, what makes you rise so early? Surely you are not still searching the forests for a gift worthy of the princess? *(Laughs)*

PIKI: No, Kuma, I am no longer searching. But I cannot talk; I must go now. *(PIKI starts to move on, but KUMA stops him roughly.)*

KUMA: The women of the village say you have no gift to bring. *(Laughs rudely)* I have fashioned gold into a necklace for Tukira.

PIKI: Yes, Kuma, I have heard of it. The whole village has heard.

KUMA: And soon Tukira will wear my necklace and become my bride. What will you bring, Piki? Perhaps a bowl of tea leaves? *(Laughs)* Or a dish of berries? *(Laughs harder)* Or perhaps the lovely princess would like a new mat woven from dried grass. *(Laughs more)* Go, Piki, and I shall meet you soon as we stand before the chieftain—unless you decide not to come. I would not blame you.

PIKI *(Passing KUMA):* I shall be there, Kuma.
(Exits, followed by KUMA, laughing. Curtain rises.)

TIME: *Later that morning.*

SETTING: *Chieftain's home.*

AT RISE: *CHIEFTAIN and TUKIRA sit side by side. 2ND GIRL combs and arranges flowers in TUKIRA's hair. MESSENGER sits behind them, tapping a drum as they talk.*

CHIEFTAIN: The morning has come, daughter. Soon the three young braves will hear the drum and arrive to present their gifts.

TUKIRA: Father, what if I cannot decide which is the most beautiful gift?

CHIEFTAIN: You will know. Your heart will tell you. And after you choose, I shall give one final test to prove the worthiness of your husband. Stand, now. Here come the youths. *(CHIEFTAIN and TUKIRA stand as DABU, KUMA, and PIKI enter, carrying gifts behind their backs. MESSENGER stops beating drum, and VILLAGE PEOPLE enter, gather around. CHIEFTAIN addresses boys.)* The three days have ended, and now Tukira will choose among you. Present your gift first, Dabu. *(DABU steps forward, kneels, holds out feathered headdress. PEOPLE murmur approval.)*

TUKIRA *(Taking headdress; with admiration):* It is lovely. Such rare feathers and such brilliant colors! Thank you, Dabu. *(TUKIRA hands headdress to 2ND GIRL. DABU rises and moves back.)*

CHIEFTAIN: Now your gift, Kuma. *(KUMA steps forward, kneels, presents necklace to TUKIRA. PEOPLE murmur even louder and lean forward for closer look. KUMA glances back at PIKI scornfully.)*

TUKIRA *(In admiring tone):* What fine gold! And such glowing topaz stones! Thank you, Kuma. *(TUKIRA hands necklace to 2ND GIRL.)*

KUMA *(Pompously):* The topaz stones do not compare to the beauty of your eyes, lovely princess. *(TUKIRA lowers her eyes, and CHIEFTAIN motions KUMA back. KUMA speaks to DABU and PIKI.)* I can see in her eyes that she admires the necklace above all else.

CHIEFTAIN: Piki, you may present your gift now.
(PIKI steps forward, kneels, presents lace mantle. PEOPLE gasp, reach forward to touch it, murmuring loudly at its beauty. TUKIRA takes mantle, unfolds it, studies it silently.)

TUKIRA *(After a moment):* Never have I held such beautiful lace. It is clearly a miracle, for no hands could spin such glistening threads and intricate patterns— so delicate yet so strong. I choose Piki's lace mantle as the best gift, Father. *(PIKI bows head gratefully, rises, steps back. KUMA scowls angrily.)*

CHIEFTAIN: You have chosen well, daughter. *(Addresses boys)* Before I give up my daughter, however, there is one final test.

KUMA *(Aside):* Aha! Perhaps I shall win yet!

CHIEFTAIN: It is said that the spirit of a great tiger roams throughout our forest. Only the wisest and noblest among the Guaranis can see the spirit. *(Motions toward audience)* Look into the forest and tell me what the tiger wears around his neck. *(PEOPLE murmur. DABU, KUMA, and PIKI gaze out silently.)*

DABU *(Questioningly):* I believe he wears around his neck a... a cord of twisted vines?

KUMA *(Boastfully):* Yes, yes, I see the spirit clearly, but you are wrong, Dabu. He wears about his neck a beaded leather strap. He turns his head now and gazes at me, recognizing me as one of the wise and noble. *(Kneels and bows toward "spirit")*

CHIEFTAIN: Piki, what can you see?

PIKI *(Puzzled):* I have looked and looked, Chieftain, but I see no tiger spirit at all. *(PEOPLE murmur.)*

CHIEFTAIN: You have shown yourself worthy, young Piki, for it is also said that the tiger spirit never reveals himself where many people are gathered. I do not know what you saw, Dabu, nor you, Kuma, but it was not the great spirit tiger. You alone, Piki, have been truthful. Surely you are the wisest and noblest of all the young Guaranis. You have competed with honor and have won the hand of my daughter in marriage. Let us make ready for the ceremony. It will be tonight.

TUKIRA: And I shall wear the lovely lace mantle for my veil.

PIKI: Yes, you shall. Just as my friend said you would. *(PIKI gently places mantle over TUKIRA's head as curtain falls.)*

THE END

149

You will answer the comprehension questions on these pages as a class.

Text Connections

1. What are the contests that Piki has to compete in to win the hand of Tukira?

2. Do you think Piki is a better person than Kuma? Explain your answer using the text for support.

3. How does this story connect to the unit theme of respect?

4. Compare how Piki treats the spider with how Shima treats the warbler in "The Origami Master."

Did You Know?

The spider is a symbol of mystery, power, and growth. There are a few types of spiders that are completely white. One of these is the crab spider.

Look Closer

Keys to Comprehension

1. Which contest does Piki win in Scene 2? What happens to Piki during the other contests?

2. Why does Piki get to marry Tukira?

3. Why does the Chieftain ask the boys about an invisible tiger?

Writer's Craft

4. How does each scene in this play build on what happened earlier?

Concept Development

5. What do the illustrations help you understand about the setting of the play?

Write

Tukira does not have a lot of say about whom she will marry. Write a story or play in which the female character has more choice about whom she will marry.

Read this letter. Then discuss it with your class.

Vocabulary Words

- **appointed**
- **assemble**
- **ceremony**
- **compete**
- **distant**
- **horizon**
- **noble**
- **prove**
- **spirit**
- **straight**
- **throughout**
- **toward**

A Trip to Ellis Island

Dear Park Director:

I would like to thank you and your excellent staff. You made my trip to Ellis Island very special. I was thrilled to see where my ancestors began their life in America.

Your staff helped me prove James Doyle came through Ellis Island. He was my great-great-grandpa. I know that he was just one of the many millions of immigrants who came to Ellis Island throughout the years. Like most of them, he insisted on leaving his home to compete for a better life in America. Ellis Island was thought of as the "golden door" to that life.

The tour guide helped me understand what James went through on the long journey. He traveled straight from Ireland toward America and spent two weeks in the dark, stuffy bottom of the ship.

I learned that as ships neared the Port of New York, passengers assembled on the deck. From there, they could see the Statue of Liberty! She stood on the distant horizon as a noble symbol of freedom. What an exciting sight it must have been for them!

When the ship landed at the appointed dock, there was no great ceremony waiting for the immigrants. They had to spend many hours getting approval to enter the country. Once the American government allowed them in, they must have felt great relief.

I am glad to know of my own link to such a historic place. When I learned about Ellis Island, I felt connected to my great-great-grandpa's spirit. I will not forget the great tour and your staff's kindness. Thank you again.

Sincerely,

Sara Doyle

Concept Vocabulary

Think about the word *integrity*. Why is it important to have integrity?

Extend Vocabulary

Write these words and their definitions in your Writer's Notebook, then list three related words next to each: *straight, noble, distant, compete.*

Read this
Social Studies
Connection.
You will answer
the questions
as a class.

Text Feature

A **pie chart** shows
the sizes or amounts
of parts that make
up the whole.

Cultural Values

The characters in "The White Spider's
Gift" are Guarani people. They are natives
of South America in what is now the
country of Paraguay. The Guarani culture
exists today. Over four million people
throughout South America speak the
Guarani language. They also have a rich
tradition of folklore and myths. "The
White Spider's Gift" gives us a look inside
the Guarani culture.

In the story, Piki is rewarded for his
behavior. He saves the white spider when
others would not. He works hard, does not
brag or cheat during the contests, and he is
noble and honest. Each of these behaviors
is a reflection of the culture's values. Stories
like this one tell how people should act.

The story has other examples of
Guarani culture. Answer each of these
questions for the Guarani in the story.
Then answer them for your own culture.

- Who are the leaders?
- What is a wedding ceremony like?
- How are older people treated?
- How are animals treated?
- How are parents treated?
- What skills do people value?
- What do people wear?

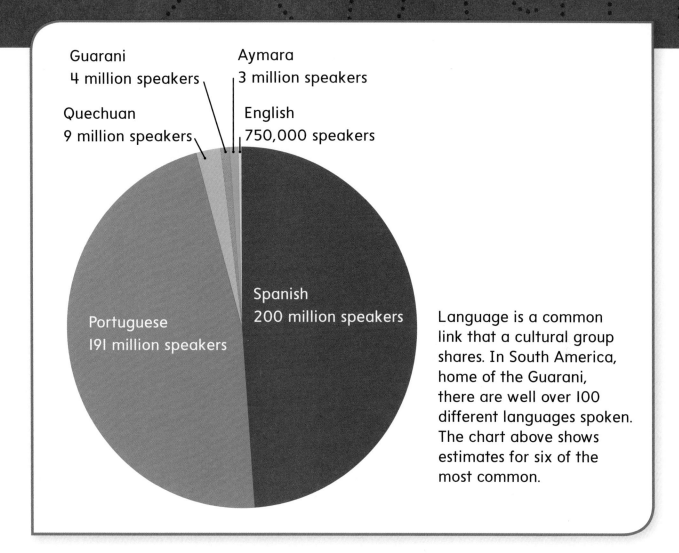

Guarani
4 million speakers

Aymara
3 million speakers

Quechuan
9 million speakers

English
750,000 speakers

Spanish
200 million speakers

Portuguese
191 million speakers

Language is a common link that a cultural group shares. In South America, home of the Guarani, there are well over 100 different languages spoken. The chart above shows estimates for six of the most common.

1. Based on what you read in "The White Spider's Gift," what are some of the values and ways of living of the Guarani culture?

2. Look at the pie chart. Are there any languages listed that are unfamiliar? Where do you think those languages originated?

3. Does Piki live up to the cultural values of the United States? Explain your answer.

 Go Digital

Search for pictures and examples of a foreign culture. How is it different from your culture?

BIG Idea

How can we prepare for weather?

Theme Connections

What aspects of life are affected by the weather?

 Background Builder Video
connected.mcgraw-hill.com

Essential Questions

How can technology help us understand weather hazards? What kinds of risks are involved in studying weather? When can it be worth it to take a risk?

Storm Chasers

by Alanna Parker

What do you do when a dangerous storm is on the way? Most people take cover. But not storm chasers. They hop in the car and go look for the storm!

Storm chasers monitor the weather closely. They travel to places where they think storms will hit. Once they arrive, they track the storms and observe them—up close. Many storm chasers take dramatic photos or videos of the storms. They may capture lightning strikes, rising floodwaters, huge hailstones, or destructive tornadoes.

Some storm chasers operate in the Midwest, the South, or other areas of the country. But many storm chasers prefer the Great Plains because that region of the United States gets the most tornadoes.

Tornado season in the Great Plains begins in April. It continues until mid-June. Storm chasers may drive hundreds of miles a day during this period, chasing violent storms across state lines. Most of the time, the chase ends without seeing a tornado. In fact, storm chasers may go weeks without catching up to a severe storm.

Chasing storms may sound unusual, but storm chasers do it for more than just the excitement. They do it for science— and to help save lives.

Are Drones the Storm Chasers of Tomorrow?

A drone is an unmanned flying vehicle. It can go places where people cannot go safely. Scientists are using drones now to study hurricanes. The drones transmit real-time data from a storm and help scientists understand how these storms form. Maybe someday they will be used on tornadoes, too.

Every year, huge storms strike cities and towns across the country. These storms—especially tornadoes—can be devastating. A tornado can be strong enough to throw a car the length of a football field. It can wreck homes or even entire towns.

Scientists are still learning about how tornadoes and other storms work. That is where storm chasers come in. Storm chasers know a lot about the weather. Many are meteorologists who have studied weather for years. The data they gather helps us understand how tornadoes form and move. This makes it easier to forecast when and where a tornado may happen.

Thunderbolt Meets Thunderstorms

A fighter jet might retire, but it doesn't always stop flying. The A-10 Thunderbolt II, a former military plane, is being refitted to chase storms. The aircraft will be flown by remote control over the storms and drop small sensors directly into the whirling winds.

Years ago, people had almost no warning time to prepare for a tornado. In 1990, the average warning time for a tornado was just 5 minutes. That's not very long! Now, the average warning time is about 13 minutes. Some of this gain is thanks to research done by storm chasers.

Sirens like this can be found across the Midwest to warn people to take shelter because a tornado or other storm is near.

Did You Know?

A tornado that occurs over water is called a waterspout. In the United States, they are most frequently found off the coast of Florida, but can also be seen on the Great Lakes. A waterspout is a serious hazard, and just like with tornados over land, people need to take precautions to avoid one.

Storm chasers also gather information not available by radar. During storms, tornadoes can form in seconds. Sometimes, they may only last for a minute or two. Radars do not scan that quickly, so they sometimes miss these short-lived tornadoes. That means that no warnings are issued. People do not know to seek safety. Luckily, storm chasers on the ground can report these tornadoes. This can help save lives.

Storm chasing can be risky. Hail, lightning, and flying objects can cause damage or injury. Storm chasers may run into floods or washed-out roads. These obstacles can trap storm chasers in the path of a tornado.

The most dangerous part, though, is usually not the violence of the storm itself, but the driving! Storm chasers may have accidents due to water, ice, or animals on the road. Other drivers cause accidents during storms, too.

Vehicles

A storm chaser's vehicle is his first line of defense. Vehicles have to be fast enough to catch a storm, but strong enough to withstand it.

Some storm chasers build a custom car from the ground up. They include special features for safety, such as:

- **Armor** – Thick, steel plates protect a car from flying debris.

- **Windows** – Windows may be made from shatterproof material.

- **Stabilizers** – Cars may have spikes, which anchor them to the ground. Some cars have "skirts." They drop down to keep wind from flowing beneath the car. These features help keep the cars from flipping over.

Vehicles like these can withstand winds of up to 250 mph!

Storm chasing can be exciting. However, storm chasing is much more than just getting in a car and running down a storm. In reality, most of a storm chaser's time is spent *not* chasing storms.

What do storm chasers do when they are not chasing storms? They analyze the data they have gathered. They take care of and repair their equipment. They learn how to use and apply new technology. They study the geography of the places where they track storms. Some storm chasers learn emergency medical and rescue techniques that can save lives. They must protect their own lives, too. They learn how to stay safe during violent storms.

Storm chasers also go to work. Most storm chasers have regular jobs. A few lucky storm chasers get paid to track storms, usually as researchers for colleges or the government. Sometimes they are part of the weather team for local or national news stations. Most storm chasers, though, do not get paid. It can cost them thousands of dollars every year to chase storms—and that happens during their vacation time from work.

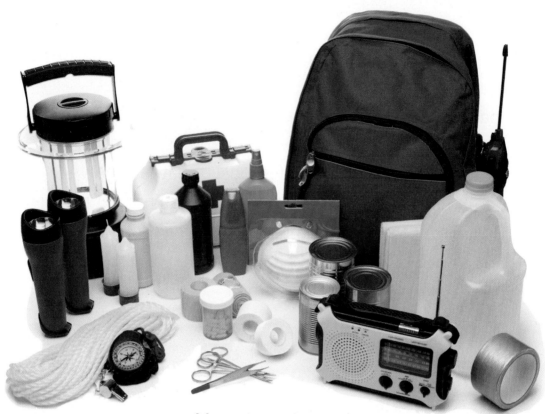

Many storm chasers carry emergency supplies with them.

Storm chasers do an important job that helps many people. They risk their lives to learn more about tornadoes and storms. The information they have collected so far has been priceless. Because of this data, the average warning time for tornadoes has more than doubled!

Storm chasers are often the first people to see a storm. When that happens, they can quickly report the storm to the local media or the National Weather Service. These groups can then warn people in the path of the storm.

Some storm chasers also help at the scene of weather disasters they witness. They may pull people out of wrecked houses. They may help treat injured people, or pass out water or blankets.

So You Want to Be a Storm Chaser?

Many storm chasers start out as "storm spotters." Storm spotters look for and report storms in their local area. You can take classes on how to be a storm spotter at your local National Weather Service office. There is also a national organization for storm spotters, called SKYWARN.

Chasing storms is not a pastime to take lightly. It is an important, and often risky, job. But for storm chasers, the risks are worth the rewards.

You will answer the comprehension questions on these pages as a class.

Text Connections

1. Why do storm chasers go looking for storms? Use evidence from the text to explain your answer.

2. What types of equipment do storm chasers need to know how to use?

3. How are storm chasers' jobs similar to what you know about the jobs of firefighters and police officers?

4. What types of extreme weather do storm chasers want to learn about?

Did You Know?

The most extreme tornado in United States' history was the Tri-State Tornado, which tore through Missouri, Illinois, and Indiana on March 18, 1925. It traveled over 219 miles and lasted three and a half hours, traveling at a speed of 73 miles per hour.

Look Closer

Keys to Comprehension

1. Why is driving usually the most dangerous part of being a storm chaser?

2. What is the main idea of this selection? List three details that support the main idea.

Writer's Craft

3. What is a DOW, or Doppler on Wheels, and why do storm chasers use it?

4. What is the key idea of each of the four sidebars?

Concept Development

5. Read the last two paragraphs on page 166. How is the information in these paragraphs connected?

Write

Be a storm chaser! Describe the most extreme weather you have ever experienced. Tell what happened before, during, and after the storm.

Read this story. Then discuss it with your class.

Vocabulary Words

- **anchor**
- **cover**
- **forecast**
- **gain**
- **hazard**
- **media**
- **mobile**
- **navigate**
- **pastime**
- **scene**
- **serious**
- **transmit**

The Big Storm

Clem Judd is an interesting man. He is smart, but also a little mysterious.

"He is quite a storyteller," Stew, the barber, always said. "He might be a little unique, but you have never met a nicer fellow."

Clem was always telling stories that could not possibly be true. People were not sure if Clem was serious or just pulling everybody's leg.

Clem had worked in the town's only bakery for thirty years. His favorite pastime was greeting customers every morning with a weather forecast. He would always smile afterward, but his forecast was never right. Clem gained a reputation for telling crazy weather stories.

Clem's favorite weather story was about the time he ventured out to sea. After fishing for a day, a big storm stranded him! His tiny ship was adrift in the large ocean. He tried to navigate his way back to land in the big storm. He hung onto his boat for three hours while the loud storm flashed lightning all around him. At one point, the whole sky was covered by storm clouds.

"For what seemed like weeks, the storm raged and I could not see. I did not know left from right!" Clem said. "It was a frightening scene!"

Using a radio, Clem tried to transmit news of his hazardous voyage to call for help. He dropped the ship's anchor to restrict the ship's mobility while he waited for help.

For two days, he survived on fish he had caught in the sea. Eventually, Clem was rescued when a helicopter spotted him. He even made it on the news after the media contacted him! But was he telling the truth? Only Clem knows!

Concept Vocabulary

Think about the word *shelter*. What are some examples of a good shelter?

Extend Vocabulary

Answer and explain the following questions. Record your answers in your Writer's Notebook.

- Which is more *serious,* a gentle spring rain or a thunderstorm? Why?
- What is a reason a bike might not be *mobile*?
- What are three things that people *navigate*?

Read this Social Studies Connection. You will answer the questions as a class.

Text Feature

A **map** shows where things are located and how to get from one place to another.

Safety First

In "Storm Chasers" you learned how people risk a lot to learn about storms. Because of the information they have collected, the average warning time for tornadoes has more than doubled. The information lets people know what to expect and how to be prepared for a potential emergency situation.

But information is not all a community needs in order to be prepared for a serious emergency. Experts have to take the information and figure out how to prepare and react. Otherwise the response to a weather hazard could be delayed or incorrect.

You may have fire drills, tornado drills, earthquake drills, or hurricane drills in your school. Experts figure out how to move a lot of people to safe cover. If a real emergency happens, everyone will know what to do.

For people who are not in school, there are no drills to practice. But in most places, laws require that buildings have plans in place in case of a weather-related emergency. These plans are made to reduce the threat of physical harm.

In case of
TORNADO

move toward

CENTRALLY LOCATED OFFICES

away from windows or other glass

TORNADO
EVACUATION PLAN

You are
HERE

Look at the two different designs for providing people with information about a building's emergency plan. Think about which design would be more effective in an emergency.

1. How does the work of storm chasers contribute to our understanding of different storms?

2. What drills have you done at your school? Are they unique to the area in which you live? Explain your answer.

3. Which of the two designs above do you think would be most effective at keeping people safe in a tornado? Why?

 Go Digital

Search for "what to do in an emergency" to learn about ways to stay safe during a potentially dangerous event. Read different sources to make sure they agree on the best steps.

Genre Informational Text

Essential Questions
How do people adjust to the changing seasons? How can weather help you relate to other people around the world?

Seasons of Change

by Jan Mader

Catching fireflies and cooking out in the summer. Picking apples and going on hay rides in the fall. Sledding and skiing in the winter. Flying kites and planting flowers in the spring. These are some of the ways people around the world enjoy the seasons.

Weather is not the same in every part of the world or even in different parts of the United States. Depending on where you live, the weather of each season can be very different. The way people experience the seasons can be very different, too.

Do you love summer? In the United States, summer is the warmest season of the year. Flowers are in full bloom, people spend lots of time outside, and the days are longer. Most children are on vacation from school. Summer begins in June and lasts for three months.

In the Midwest, the hot sun and long days help garden vegetables and farm crops grow. You can pick tomatoes, peppers, and green beans, right from your backyard! Farmer's markets start popping up everywhere to sell fresh produce.

August

Location	Average High Temperature	Average Precipitation
Concord, NH	81°F	3.1" rain
Columbus, OH	84°F	3.3" rain
Orlando, FL	92°F	7.1" rain
Fargo, ND	81°F	2.5" rain
San Diego, CA	76°F	.10" rain
San Antonio, TX	96°F	2" rain

August

Location	Average High Temperature	Average Precipitation
Moscow, Russia	71°F	3.2" rain
Oslo, Norway	68°F	3.5" rain
Nairobi, Kenya	73°F	.9" rain
Beijing, China	85°F	6.2" rain

Parts of the United States are hotter and drier than the Midwest. The hottest place in the summer is Death Valley, California. The temperature can reach 134 degrees Fahrenheit. The average summer rainfall is less than two inches. Now that is hot and dry!

Florida is another hot place, but people still vacation there in the summer. Why? They visit amusement parks and flock to the beaches. The ocean water is warm and fun for swimming. But watch out for afternoon storms! Unlike the desert, Florida summers can be rainy and humid.

June marks the first month of summer in Russia also. Russia can be very warm in the summer. Russian people go to parks and other green places to escape the sun's heat. Some people go to the countryside in the summer for relief. If they are lucky, they may own a summer cottage. A cottage is a great place for a Russian family to get away from the heat of the city!

As summer ends in the United States, autumn blows in with gusto! The weather changes. Leaves turn bright colors and fall from the trees. The air begins to get chilly and the days get shorter. Children go back to school. Autumn begins in September and is three months long.

The New England states are famous for their beautiful early autumn leaves. People travel from miles away to see the colorful fall display. The weather is crisp and cool. It is perfect for long hikes and picking apples. Some people say that New England has the best autumn of all!

November

Location	Average Low Temperature	Average Precipitation
Concord, NH	28°F	3.7" rain
Columbus, OH	36°F	3.2" rain
Orlando, FL	58°F	2.1" rain
Fargo, ND	20°F	7.9" snow
San Diego, CA	69°F	1.0" rain
San Antonio, TX	50°F	2.2" rain

While people in New England are enjoying a refreshing autumn, people in some parts of Texas are still roasting hot! In San Antonio, Texas, the temperature may still rise over 90°F. The leaves on most trees do not change color, so people who live in San Antonio can visit Lost Maples State Natural Area. Lost Maples is named after the maple trees that cover some hillsides west of San Antonio. Cooler temperatures cause the leaves to turn beautiful shades of yellow and orange.

San Antonio has many floods in the autumn. Unlike the New England cities that get rain off and on all year, San Antonio gets most of its rain in a few large storms. The ground is hard from long summer droughts, which causes much of the water to run off the top of the ground instead of soaking in. This results in flooded rivers and streets.

November

Location	Average Low Temperature	Average Precipitation
Moscow, Russia	26°F	2.1" rain
Oslo, Norway	29°F	1.6" snow
Nairobi, Kenya	55°F	5.8" rain
Beijing, China	32°F	.2" rain

Autumn is beautiful in China. The extreme heat of the summer dissipates and the comfortable weather lasts until November. Native gingko trees line many streets. Their leaves turn bright yellow and can turn sidewalks into golden paths. The Chinese people celebrate a holiday called the Mid-Autumn Festival. During this festival, they also celebrate the full harvest moon. October 1 is another holiday. It is China's National Day. Children get several days out of school and adults take time off work. No wonder the Chinese people like autumn!

Winter follows autumn. Of all the seasons, winter is the one that people tend to either love or hate. People who love winter usually like to ski, sled, or participate in other outdoor winter activities. People who hate winter dislike the cold and the feeling of being cooped up inside. In winter, the days are short and the nights are long. Do you like winter?

North Dakota is a northern Great Plains state. Its winters can be harsh. Cold and gusty winds, blizzards, and even whiteouts are not uncommon. Snow drifts can block roads so that schools and businesses close.

January

Location	Average Low Temperature	Average Precipitation
Concord, NH	10°F	18" snow
Columbus, OH	22°F	9.2" snow
Orlando, FL	49°F	2.3" rain
Fargo, ND	0°F	11.2" snow
San Diego, CA	49°F	1.9" rain
San Antonio, TX	40°F	1.7" rain

January

Location	Average Low Temperature	Average Precipitation
Moscow, Russia	15°F	16" snow
Oslo, Norway	19°F	5.5" snow
Nairobi, Kenya	60°F	2.2" rain
Beijing, China	17°F	.10" rain

Some people plan winter vacations just to visit the snow. They go where the air is cold and the land is frozen. Mountains are a great place for ski vacations. Ski resorts can be found in many regions of the United States. Heavy snowfall in the Rocky Mountains makes Colorado a great place for winter sports.

Be on the lookout for avalanches. An avalanche is a sudden, rapid flow of snow down a hill or a mountain. Avalanches bury everything in their paths. Avalanches usually happen before or after a snowstorm. The high winds move the snow and make it unstable. Skiers beware! It is easier to stay away from an avalanche than to get out of one.

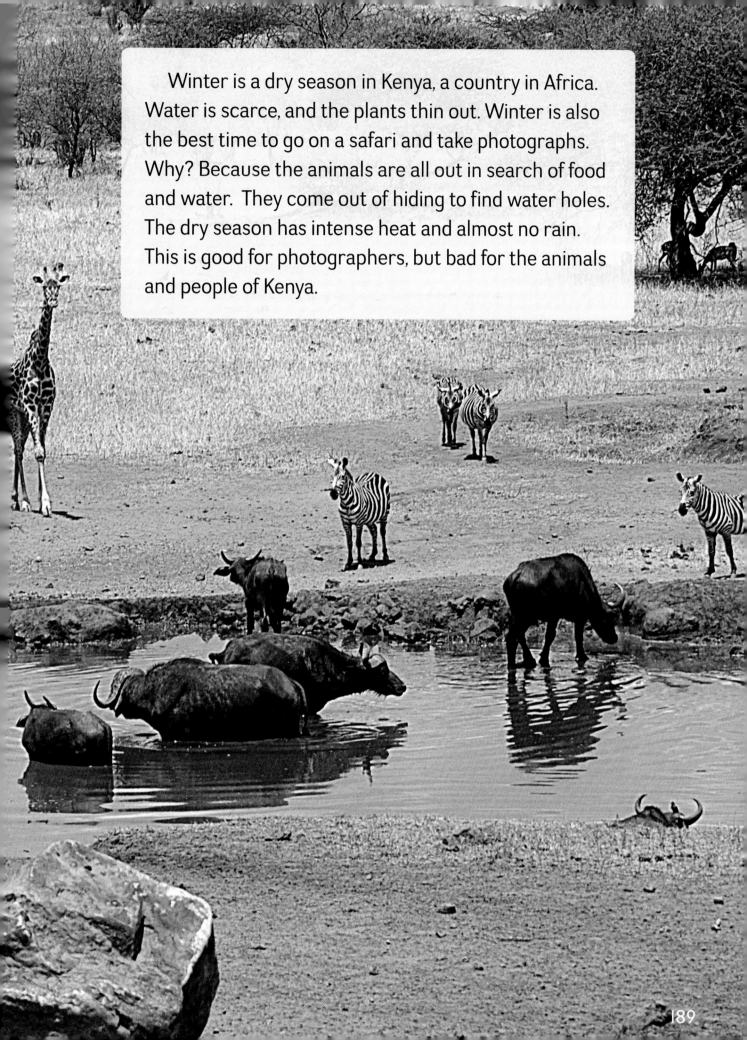

Winter is a dry season in Kenya, a country in Africa. Water is scarce, and the plants thin out. Winter is also the best time to go on a safari and take photographs. Why? Because the animals are all out in search of food and water. They come out of hiding to find water holes. The dry season has intense heat and almost no rain. This is good for photographers, but bad for the animals and people of Kenya.

Are you glad when winter is over? Spring is the season when things come alive again. Fawns are born. Tulips and daffodils sprout from gardens. The sun shines. The farmers get their fields ready to plant crops. Spring is a happy time of year.

The sun rises earlier in the morning and sets later at night, providing more heat to the ground. This creates warm, moist air that generates powerful winds and increases precipitation. As the saying goes: March winds and April showers bring forth May flowers.

But those March winds can be violent. In Chicago, one March gust of wind was recorded at 52 miles per hour. Luckily, March leads to April and May.

May

Location	Average High Temperature	Average Precipitation
Concord, NH	68°F	3.6" rain
Columbus, OH	73°F	4.1" rain
Orlando, FL	88°F	3.4" rain
Fargo, ND	70°F	2.8" rain
San Diego, CA	68°F	.10" rain
San Antonio, TX	87°F	4" rain

May

Location	Average High Temperature	Average Precipitation
Moscow, Russia	65°F	1.9" rain
Oslo, Norway	60°F	2" rain
Nairobi, Kenya	74°F	7.4" rain
Beijing, China	79°F	1.3" rain

In most parts of the United States, spring brings lots of rain. The spring sun and rain are all it takes to make the tulips in Holland, Michigan, bloom like a colorful painting. People come from all over the world just to see the tulips.

Along with the beautiful flowers come the spring thunderstorms. Thunderstorms almost always have lightning, thunder, wind, and rain. Thunderstorms can bring soccer games to a halt. They can ruin family picnics. It is not safe to be outside during a thunderstorm.

Sometimes, tornadoes accompany thunderstorms. Tornadoes have fast-spinning winds that can be dangerous. Some states, like Oklahoma, get lots of tornadoes in the spring.

Spring in Norway is spectacular. The trees and flowers come alive. The snow in the mountains melts and waterfalls gush down the mountainsides.

Northern Norway is much cooler than southern Norway. The temperatures can change quickly during spring in the mountains. If you want to hike in Norway in the spring, be prepared. What starts out as a warm day can quickly turn cold.

Lots of festivals in Norway take place in the spring, so there is always plenty to do. May 17 is Norway's National Day. Children carry banners and flags during National Day parades.

What season do you like best? How does the weather affect you during each season? How does the weather change? It can be fun to live in a place where the seasons are quite varied. By the time you are ready to stop feeling the heat of summer, autumn blows in and cools you off! After a harsh winter, you can look forward to a warm spring and the new life it brings. The seasons are all exciting in unique ways. Enjoy the seasons, but be prepared for the weather they bring!

Something Told the Wild Geese

by Rachel Field

Essential Questions

Why do some birds fly south for the winter?
How does the weather affect animals?

Something told the wild geese
It was time to go,
Though the fields lay golden
Something whispered, "snow."

Leaves were green and stirring,
Berries, luster-glossed,
But beneath warm feathers
Something cautioned, "frost."

All the sagging orchards
Steamed with amber spice,
But each wild breast stiffened
At remembered ice.

Something told the wild geese
It was time to fly,
Summer sun was on their wings,
Winter in their cry.

Genre Informational Text

Essential Question

How can weather impact your community? What are ways we can protect ourselves from weather we cannot control?

Tornadoes!

by Gail Gibbons

It is raining hard; the winds are strong.
The sky is dark. Suddenly a twisting column
of moist air reaches down from a cloud and
touches the ground. It makes a loud, roaring
sound. It is a tornado!

Tornadoes begin inside storm clouds
called cumulonimbus (KYOOM-yoo-low-NIM-
bus) clouds, which are made up of warm,
moist air. These large, dark clouds can grow
to be tall and enormous. There is lightning,
thunder, rain, hail, and high winds.

A THUNDERHEAD is a very large, dark cumulonimbus cloud or group of cumulonimbus clouds.

CONDENSATION occurs when moist, warm air cools and turn into a liquid such as rain.

UPDRAFT

DOWNDRAFT

HEAT ALWAYS RISES

When warm, humid air rises from the ground toward a dark cumulonimbus thunderhead, it creates an updraft that pulls more warm, humid air with it. When the air rises to where the temperature is cooler, condensation occurs, creating rain or hail. The cool air falls back toward Earth, creating a downdraft.

Tornadoes may occur at any time of the year if the weather conditions are right.

If the updraft and the downdraft come together and start to spin, a funnel-shaped cloud forms inside the thunderhead and sometimes tilts into a funnel that reaches down toward the ground.

As the funnel cloud spins faster and faster, it sucks up more and more warm air and becomes bigger and louder and more powerful. If it touches the ground, a tornado is born.

The letter *F* represents *Fujita*

The letter *E* represents *Enhanced*

EF-0

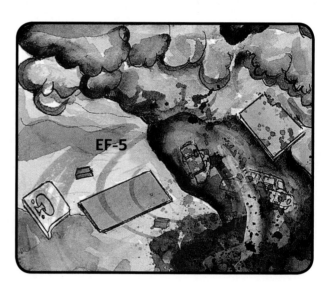

EF-5

In 1971, T. Theodore Fujita developed the Fujita Tornado Scale, rating tornadoes on a scale from F0 to F5. Since then the scale has been enhanced, setting stricter standards for measuring damage. Starting February 1, 2007, the Enhanced Fujita Tornado Scale has been used to classify tornadoes from EF-0 to EF-5.

Classifications are mostly based on the amount and type of damage caused. There is no way yet to directly measure the winds in every tornado. Wind speeds are estimates only and are based on the severity of the damage. No matter how big or little a tornado is or how long it lasts on the ground, it is likely to cause damage.

Enhanced Fujita Tornado Scale

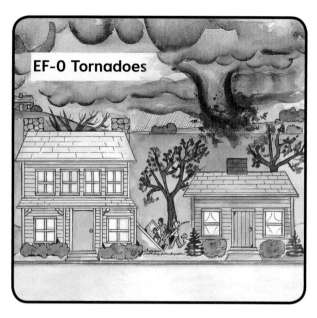

EF-0 tornadoes may have wind speeds between 65 mph (104.6 kph) and 85 mph (136.8 kph).

They can damage chimneys, break limbs off trees, and blow over shallow-rooted trees.

EF-1 tornadoes may have wind speeds between 86 mph (138.4 kph) and 110 mph (177 kph).

They can peel the surface off roofs and overturn small trucks and mobile homes.

EF-2 tornadoes may have wind speeds between 111 mph (178.6 kph) and 136 mph (218.9 kph).

They can tear the whole roof off a frame house, demolish mobile homes, and snap or uproot large trees.

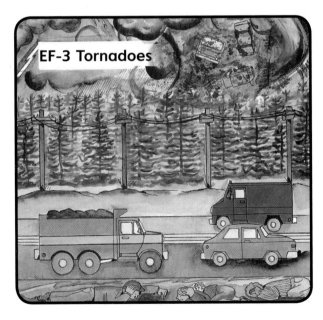

EF-3 tornadoes may have wind speeds between 137 mph (220.5 kph) and 166 mph (267.1 kph).

They can uproot a forest and lift heavy cars off the ground.

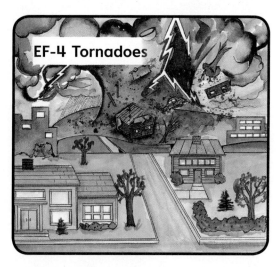

EF-4 tornadoes may have wind speeds between 167 mph (268.8 kph) and 200 mph (321.9 kph).

They can demolish well-constructed houses, leaving few walls standing. Other structures may be blown off their foundations and moved some distance.

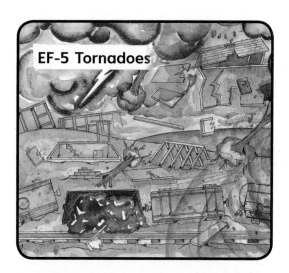

EF-5 tornadoes are the most violent tornadoes. They may have wind speeds of 201 mph (323.5 kph) and more.

Well-constructed houses are lifted off their foundations, carried away, and totally destroyed. Trains have been lifted off their tracks. The devastation is so extreme that it is hard to believe.

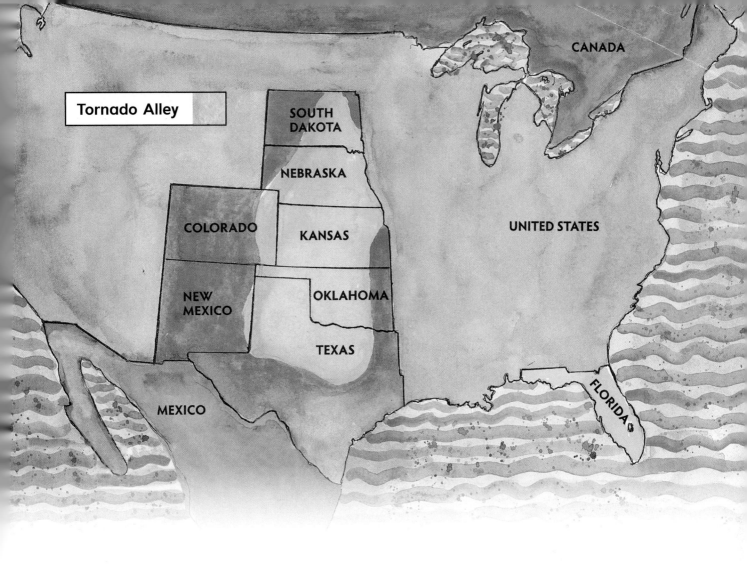

There are two regions in the United States that experience tornadoes frequently. One region is in the middle section of the country, where most of the violent tornadoes occur. It is often referred to as Tornado Alley. In this area most of the tornadoes occur during April, May, and June.

The other is the state of Florida, where most tornadoes occur during January, February, and March. The United States has about 1,200 tornadoes a year, more than any other country.

METEOROLOGISTS are scientists who study weather.

Meteorologists are on constant watch to predict and warn people of dangerous storms that may produce tornadoes. They study computer data and radar screens.

The National Weather Service reports to television and radio stations if they see the possibility of tornadoes forming. This information is broadcasted every 15 minutes to give people some time to prepare.

What to Do When a Tornado Approaches

If your house has a basement, go to it at once.

If you are in a house without a basement, go to an interior closet or bathroom far from the outside walls.

Crouch down low and cover your head with your hands. Stay away from windows and outside walls.

Try to cover yourself with a mattress or heavy blankets for protection from falling debris.

If you can, crouch under a set of stairs.

If you are in a car, get out immediately! Try to find a low spot, such as a ditch, to lie in. Lie flat on your stomach and cover your head with your hands.

After the tornado, be careful of fallen electrical wires, broken glass, and unsafe structures.

Try to have an adult help you!

You will answer the comprehension questions on these pages as a class.

Text Connections

1. How do tornadoes form?
2. What is the difference between an EF-0 tornado and an EF-5?
3. What does *enhanced* mean? How do you know?
4. Does the text in "Tornadoes!" agree with any of the information you read about in "Seasons of Change"?

Did You Know?

On March 12, 2006, a teenager from southwest Missouri was carried almost one-quarter mile by a tornado. And he lived to tell about it!

Look Closer

Keys to Comprehension

1. Why do more tornadoes happen in the middle of the United States in the spring?

2. Look at the instructions on pages 216–217 for what to do if a tornado approaches. What steps would you take if a tornado approached your home?

Writer's Craft

3. What are some scientific terms the author uses in "Tornadoes!"? What do they mean, and why do you think the author uses these technical terms instead of easier words?

Concept Development

4. How do the illustrations of the Enhanced Fujita Tornado Scale help you understand tornadoes?

5. "Tornadoes!" and "Storm Chasers" are both about extreme weather. How are the main ideas of each similar? How are they different?

Write

Explain why you should go to the basement or an interior closet or bathroom during a tornado.

219

Read this story. Then discuss it with your class.

Vocabulary Words

- classifications
- demolish
- funnel cloud
- prepare
- radar
- updraft

At the Science Museum

"Rita, we have to leave in five minutes!" my dad called out as he finished preparing my lunch for school. Today, my class was going on a field trip to the science museum!

When I got to school, Mrs. Chapman was already gathering the class to get onto the bus. I quickly grabbed my notebook and got in line.

At the museum, we were met by Alberto, our tour guide. He told us that we would first be learning about tornadoes. Alberto told our class that tornadoes start as funnel clouds. Clouds form into a funnel shape, which can turn into a tornado. He said that tornadoes can cause serious damage.

"Can a tornado demolish a house?" Kenny asked.

Alberto nodded his head yes. "Tornadoes are classified by their strength. Strong tornadoes can demolish or even pick up entire houses! The damage is caused by the updraft, or the air that forces objects up and into the tornado."

Kenny looked surprised. We all did.

"Tornadoes can even carry cars for miles," Alberto told us.

Mrs. Chapman led the class to the next exhibit. Soon we heard loud thunder coming from outside.

"It's beginning to storm," Mrs. Chapman said.

Alberto left us to check the radar, which shows in which direction storms are traveling. When he returned, he had good news.

"The storm will pass soon," Alberto said.

After learning about destructive tornadoes, the class was happy to hear that good news.

Concept Vocabulary

Think about the word *precautions*. What are some examples of precautions people take?

Extend Vocabulary

Answer and explain the following questions. Record your answers in your Writer's Notebook.

- What kind of people, places, or things might use *radar*? Why?
- Why is it important to *prepare* for a test?
- If you see a *funnel cloud*, what should you do?

Read this
Social Studies
Connection.
You will answer
the questions
as a class.

Text Feature

A **sidebar** is an
added section on
the page that gives
more information.

Rebuilding Together

In "Tornadoes!" you learned that when a tornado occurs, houses, barns, schools, and even whole towns can be demolished. The more people in an area, the more damage is done. Rescue efforts are very important in helping people find shelter, food, and clothing. Communities that experience a devastating tornado also need support in rebuilding.

Organizations like The American Red Cross are always prepared to respond to disasters. They use mobile headquarters to hand out food, open shelters, and provide health services. Federal and state governments also provide disaster relief. This may be in the form of loans or grants to help people and communities rebuild.

Other countries may or may not have the same resources. When a tornado destroys communities in other countries, the rest of the world often comes to help out. The International Red Cross and the Red Crescent Societies were founded to help people all across the world. They also coordinate with governments. This is one way that governments and people help each other in different parts of the world.

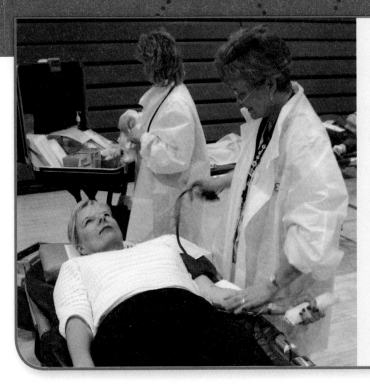

Many people donate blood during a disaster. Blood donations help save lives and are quick and easy to do. The United States has around 9.2 million blood donors every year. Blood donors in the United States give more than 15 million individual donations each year!

1. How is the information in the sidebar related to the main text? Why do you think it is separated?

2. What are some ways you and the people and groups in your community could help a different country that has experienced a large natural disaster?

3. Many people and organizations come together to help rebuild after a disaster. What are other reasons for individuals and groups to come together and cooperate?

 Go Digital

Search for "tornadoes around the world" and "Red Cross" to find out about the different places where tornadoes occur and the damage they can cause. Find pictures for a collage to show people helping.

Genre Play

Essential Questions

What are some jobs related to weather? What can scientists do to better predict weather? How does predicting weather improve our lives?

Get the Facts

by Sheila Hernandez
illustrated by Angela Adams

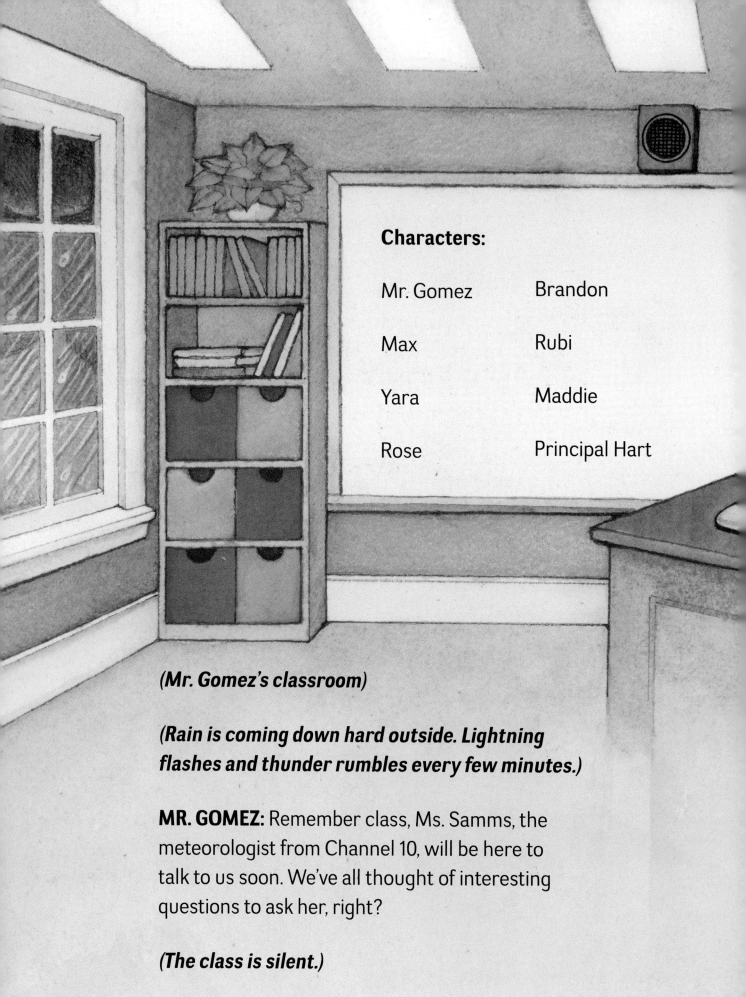

Characters:

Mr. Gomez	Brandon
Max	Rubi
Yara	Maddie
Rose	Principal Hart

(Mr. Gomez's classroom)

(Rain is coming down hard outside. Lightning flashes and thunder rumbles every few minutes.)

MR. GOMEZ: Remember class, Ms. Samms, the meteorologist from Channel 10, will be here to talk to us soon. We've all thought of interesting questions to ask her, right?

(The class is silent.)

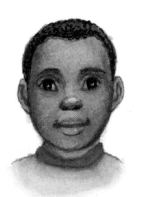

MR. GOMEZ: Anybody?

MAX: *(looking out the window at the lightning)* How about, can she tell us how long this storm will last?

YARA: Yeah. I'd like to know if it will still be raining this afternoon. I have a soccer game and I don't want it to get cancelled.

MR. GOMEZ: Well, meteorologists use many tools to forecast thunderstorms and other weather. Radar can help them see inside a thunderstorm and tell how strong it is. Radar also gives them an idea of how long a storm will last.

RUBI: So she can tell us whether Yara will be able to play her soccer game?

MR. GOMEZ: Ms. Samms could tell us if her predictions suggest that the storm will be gone in time for the game. But things might not turn out the way she predicts.

MADDIE: She's on television. Shouldn't her predictions be right?

MR. GOMEZ: Meteorology cannot make perfect predictions. Earth's climate and weather are very complicated. But as the instruments meteorologists use to measure weather become more accurate, their predictions improve.

227

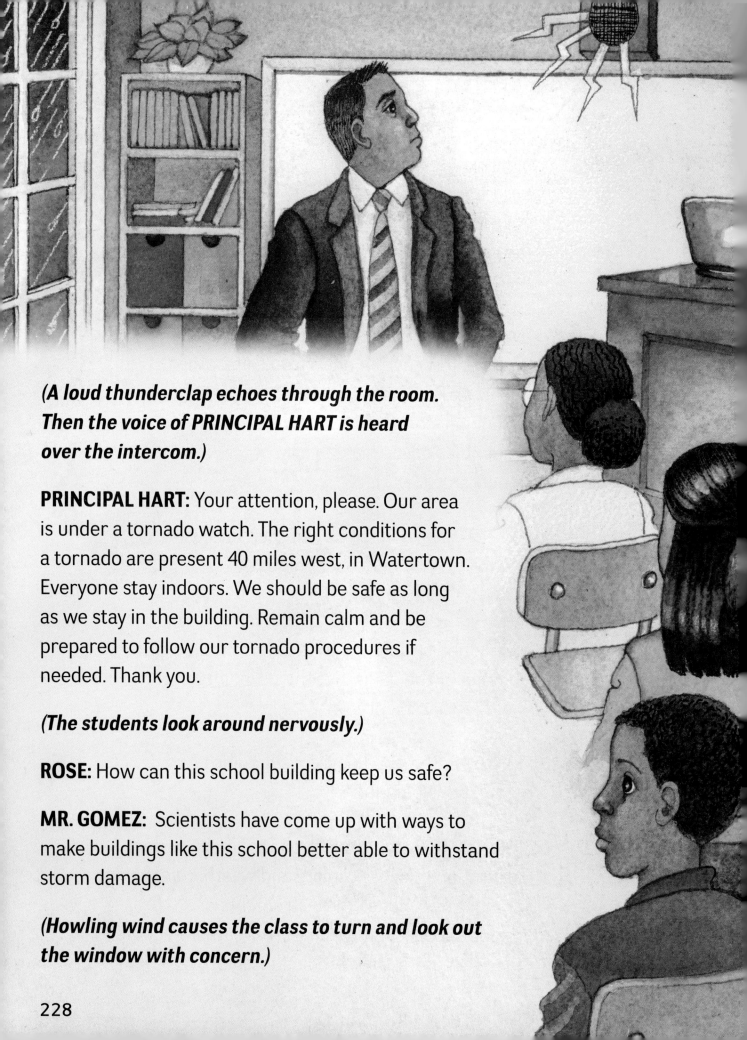

(A loud thunderclap echoes through the room. Then the voice of PRINCIPAL HART is heard over the intercom.)

PRINCIPAL HART: Your attention, please. Our area is under a tornado watch. The right conditions for a tornado are present 40 miles west, in Watertown. Everyone stay indoors. We should be safe as long as we stay in the building. Remain calm and be prepared to follow our tornado procedures if needed. Thank you.

(The students look around nervously.)

ROSE: How can this school building keep us safe?

MR. GOMEZ: Scientists have come up with ways to make buildings like this school better able to withstand storm damage.

(Howling wind causes the class to turn and look out the window with concern.)

MR. GOMEZ: We had a wind-resistant roof installed for situations exactly like this. That should help keep the building secure, but we will still need to take precautions if the storm gets worse.

BRANDON: My mom is an engineer and she works for a company that designs shatter-resistant glass. She said our school had it installed in every classroom just last year. That should help keep us safe, right?

MR. GOMEZ: Right, though tornadoes are still very dangerous. If we get a tornado warning, meaning that a tornado has actually been spotted, we will do what we have practiced in our drills. Remember, first we move away from the windows and outside walls, close to the board. Then we squat low and cover our heads with our arms.

(The students still look concerned but nod.)

YARA: Ms. Samms isn't coming here now, right?

GOMEZ: I don't know. Ms. Samms will probably have her hands full now with this tornado watch.

MAX: Why? *(laughing)* Does she fight tornadoes?

MR. GOMEZ: In a way, she does fight tornadoes. Because meteorologists like Ms. Samms study the weather, people have been warned, and now they have time to find shelter.

MAX: Why can't they tell us exactly where the tornado will hit and when?

MR. GOMEZ: Tornadoes are not stable systems. They are difficult to predict. But scientists are studying tornadoes, past and present, looking for patterns. This will help improve the accuracy of their predictions.

ROSE: Is there any way to prevent tornadoes from happening at all?

MR. GOMEZ: Unfortunately, no. Weather is a part of the natural world, but we can try to think of new ways to minimize the danger that extreme weather poses. Maybe some of you will one day come up with a solution that helps to save people from weather-related hazards.

(After a knock on the door, PRINCIPAL HART enters.)

PRINCIPAL HART: I just received a message from Channel 10. Ms. Samms has been called to the station to report on the tornado watch, but she will definitely be here tomorrow.

(PRINCIPAL HART exits.)

MR. GOMEZ: *(to the class)* Maybe it's not a bad thing that Ms. Samms won't be here today. Now we can come up with some better questions about predicting tornadoes and reducing the threat they pose.

(Class gets to work researching tornadoes and preparing questions for Ms. Samms.)

Winter Dance

by Linda Kao
illustrated by Maria Mola

Whisper snowflakes spin and swirl,
They pull me in to twist and twirl.
The wind is music, low and sweet,
The drums, the crunch beneath my feet.
Leaping, I forget the cold,
There's only dancing,
bright and bold!

Essential Question
How do you feel when you think
about each of the seasons?

Spring Wind

by Lucy Ford
illustrated by Julia Sarcone-Roach

On a chilly night, a warm wind blows.
Little by little, it melts the snow.
Outside my window, the whole wood drips:
Tap, tap, tap and *ploppity-plip.*
The trees were white when I went to bed,
But spring has come when I lift my head.

Summer Is Here

by Theodore James

Summer is here!
It's the hottest time of year.
The sun is blazing bright
and the sky is blue and clear.

Summer is here!
It's a stormy time of year.
When thunder follows lightning,
rain clouds must be near.

Summer is here!
Let's enjoy this time of year.
The storm has passed,
so let's go outside
and play and run and cheer!

Autumn Colors

by Emily Hill

Leaves of red, rust, and gold
float one by one
through cool, crisp air
to pile up in the grass
and on the sidewalks.
Summer's heat has faded
into fall's chill.
Late in the season
silver frost on the lawns
cloud of breath in air
means winter is near.

You will answer the comprehension questions on these pages as a class.

Text Connections

1. In "Get the Facts" why is Ms. Samms coming to talk to Mr. Gomez's class?

2. Why is it difficult for the people who predict the weather to be exact?

3. What is the difference between a tornado watch and a tornado warning? Use evidence from the text to explain your answer.

4. How does Ms. Samms' job compare to that of the scientists in "Storm Chasers"?

Did You Know?

Most tornadoes occur in the afternoon because the ground and air are warmest at that time of day. So it is a good idea for schools to be prepared in case of a tornado.

Look Closer

Keys to Comprehension

1. How have the students prepared for a tornado warning?

2. Do you think the students are very interested in weather at the start of the play? Does their attitude change by the end?

Writer's Craft

3. If you were going to divide this play into two scenes, where would the first scene end and why?

4. Compare the speaker in "Winter Dance" to the speaker in "Summer Is Here." How do they feel about the weather they are describing? How do your feelings about the weather they are describing differ from the speakers'?

Concept Development

5. How does the illustration of Mr. Gomez on page 229 help you understand what to do if there is a tornado warning?

Write

Make a list of steps to follow in a tornado drill.

Read this story. Then discuss it with your class.

Vocabulary Words

- **accurate**
- **concern**
- **instruments**
- **meteorologist**
- **minimize**
- **threat**

Watching the Weather

I grabbed the camera as Angelo stood at the edge of the road with his microphone. He was almost ready to report.

"I am concerned that the rain will make it hard to see you," I shouted. If I was not loud, he would not hear me over the sound of the wind.

The islands were having bad storms again. The news station sent us to cover the weather. The meteorologists at the station did not think the storms would threaten our safety, so we drove around to record live coverage.

Angelo ran back to the van to grab a weather instrument that measured wind speed.

"The wind is blowing 30 miles per hour!" Angelo exclaimed. He needed to accurately measure the wind speed. When he reported, he wanted to tell the facts.

Angelo also wanted to minimize any fears that people might have. The rain and wind were not expected to cause damage.

"Here comes the rain," I told Angelo as he quickly put the tool back. He stepped in front of the camera, held up his microphone, and began to speak.

"I'm Angelo Santos, and I'm here on the north side of the island reporting on the rain and high winds," Angelo told the camera.

Just then, rain began to pour down. It soaked us along with the camera. Angelo laughed as he tried to talk over the rain. I could not hear him!

As the rain fell even harder, I signaled "Cut!" and ran back to the van as Angelo followed close behind.

Concept Vocabulary

Think about the word *alert*. What are different kinds of alerts? What do they warn of?

Extend Vocabulary

Copy the word web into your Writer's Notebook. Then fill it in with three antonyms and three synonyms for *accurate*.

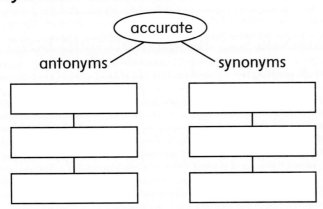

Read this Social Studies Connection. You will answer the questions as a class.

Text Feature

A **caption** tells about a picture and adds information to an article or story.

Wind and Energy

While the howling winds of a tornado are scary, not all wind is a threat. In fact, wind has been an important tool of human civilization for thousands of years.

What makes the wind blow? It's the sun! The sun heats our planet, but because some areas receive more sunlight than others, the heat is uneven. The difference in temperatures causes wind.

Winds create energy that can be very useful to people. The Egyptians used wind power to sail their ships on the Nile River. Also, people discovered that they could use windmills to grind grains on farms. Wherever the environment produces a lot of wind, people have found ways to use it.

Today, wind power is also used to create electricity. Since the late 1900s, wind farms have been built all around the world to satisfy the demand for electricity. Large wind farms contain hundreds of wind turbines, or modern windmills.

Concerns for the environment have caused people to think more about using wind power. Because wind is a renewable energy source, researchers believe that wind power will continue to grow in the United States.

A modern wind farm in the United States.

1. How does the environment of a place determine whether the people who live there can use wind power?

2. Look up the word *renewable* in the dictionary. What do you think a renewable energy source is?

3. Look at the above photograph and the caption under it. How does the caption help you understand the photograph?

 Go Digital

Find more information about how wind is created and how wind power is used throughout the world.

Hot Enough to

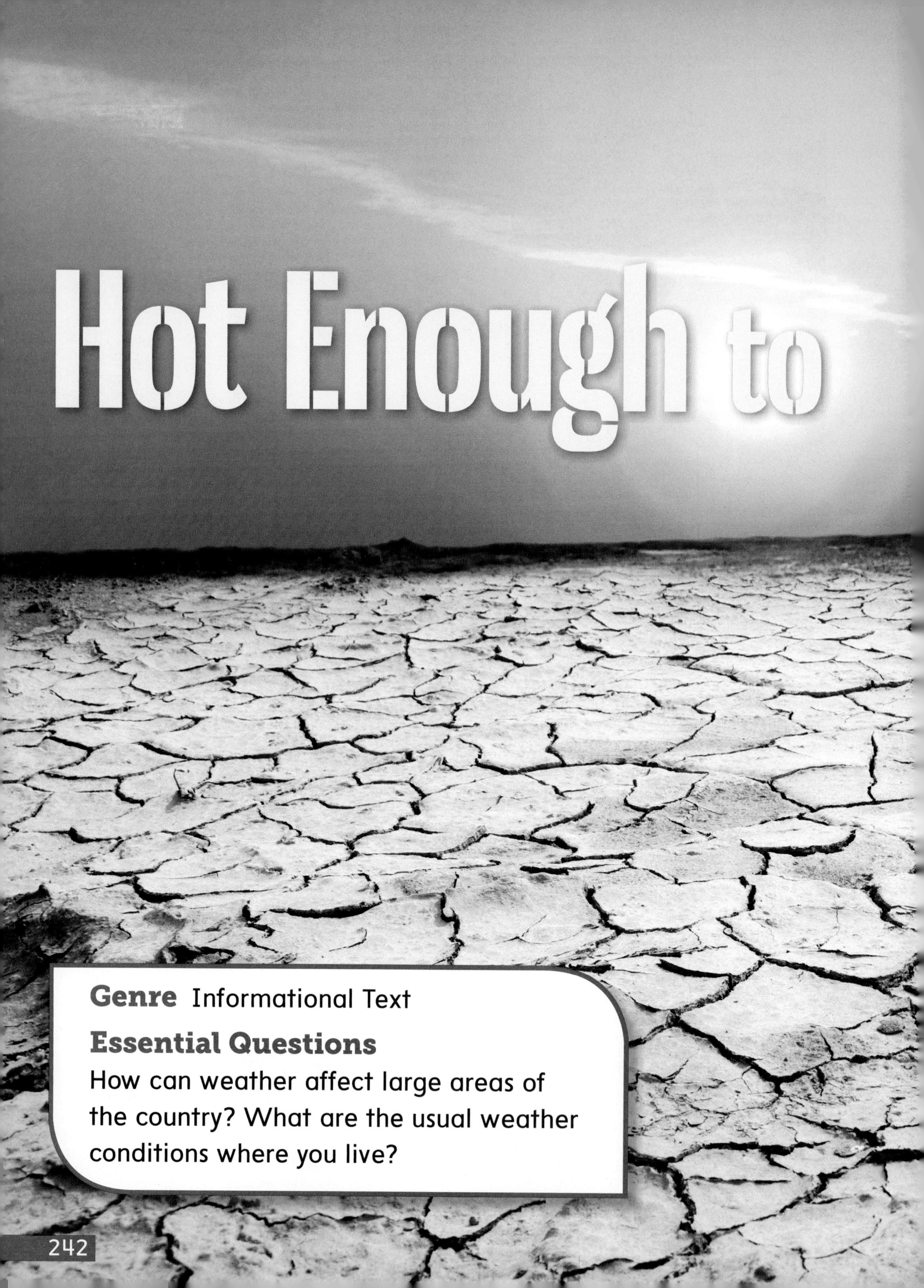

Genre Informational Text

Essential Questions

How can weather affect large areas of the country? What are the usual weather conditions where you live?

Fry an EGG

by Raymond Huber

Temperatures in the Mojave Desert vary widely from low to high. The mountainous area in the north can be extremely cold. But in the south it can be extremely hot.

The seasons are extreme, too. In the summer, temperatures climb above 100°F, but winter can have temperatures below freezing.

The Sierra Nevada mountains in the Mojave Desert can be covered in snow in winter.

CHAPTER 2 Dry as a Bone

Desert Waters

Only about five inches of rain falls in the Mojave Desert each year. The hot winds quickly dry up any water, but there are still washes and springs.

Washes are just dry stream beds for much of the year. These washes can fill up quickly if it rains though. Sometimes washes make deep channels in the land.

Desert springs are places where underground water comes up to the surface. The water makes the ground more fertile. It is easier for plants to grow near springs.

Rain Shadow

Why is the Mojave Desert so dry? It is dry because the Sierra Nevada mountains make a "rain shadow" over the Mojave Desert.

Wind pushes moist air from the Pacific Ocean up to the Sierra Nevadas. But the mountains act like a wall. They force the moist air to rise.

As it rises over the mountains, the air cools and drops most of its water as rain.

The now-dry air passes over the mountains. As it sinks, it warms. It rushes down the other side and blows into the Mojave Desert as a hot, dry wind.

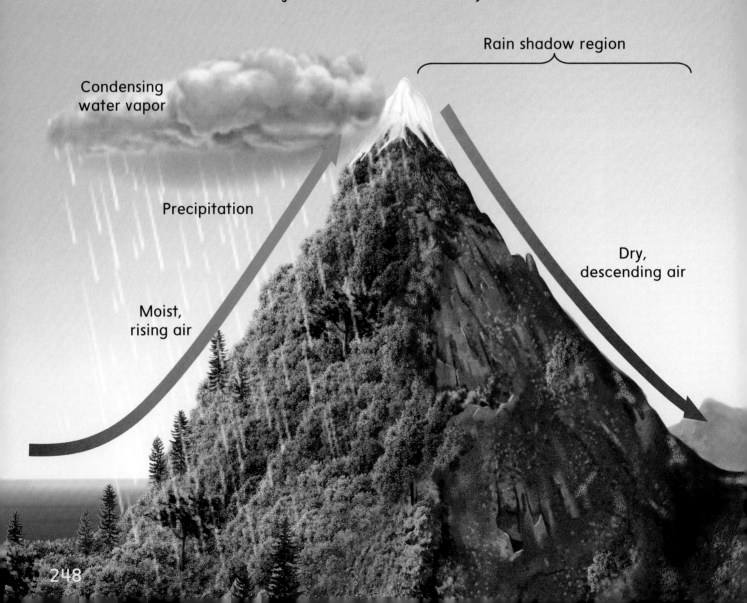

Rain shadow region

Condensing
water vapor

Precipitation

Moist,
rising air

Dry,
descending air

Heat That Dries Out Earth

The Mojave Desert is a very warm place for most of the year. In the summer the temperature averages between 90°F and 105°F. The ground gets even hotter than the air.

The hot daytime temperatures in the Mojave cause water to change quickly to vapor. Rain, rivers, and water in the soil all evaporate in the extreme heat.

What Is Evaporation?

When it rains, a puddle can form on the ground. When the sun comes out, it heats the ground and the water in the puddle. As the water heats up, it changes into a gas called water vapor. The water vapor floats up into the air. It forms clouds and may fall again as rain.

The Extreme Heat of the Sun

Why does it get so hot in the desert? One reason is that there are very few clouds. There is nothing to block the sun's heat. The sunlight hits the ground and the rocks. Then it bounces back up again, which makes things even hotter.

Deserts have very few clouds to protect them from the sun.

The Most Extreme

Death Valley is probably the most extreme part of the Mojave Desert.

The valley is 140 miles long and is the lowest point in the United States: it is 282 feet below sea level.

It is incredibly dry and hot in Death Valley. In most of the Mojave, temperatures can reach a little over 100°F. But in Death Valley, the air temperature can reach 134°F. At ground level it gets up to a sizzling 165°F. That's hot enough to fry an egg!

This salty crust can be more than three feet thick.

Death Valley monkeyflower

Salt Creek pupfish

Death Valley averages less than two inches of rain each year. Parts of the valley floor are covered with a crust of salt. What caused this? Years ago, the area that is now Death Valley was covered by water. Over time, the area became warmer. When the water began to dry up, it left behind salt and other minerals.

It might seem that nothing could survive in a place called Death Valley, but many animals and plants can. Some, such as the Salt Creek pupfish or the Death Valley monkeyflower, are found nowhere else in the world.

CHAPTER 4 Two More U.S. Deserts

The Sonoran Desert

The Mojave Desert is only one desert in the United States. South of it is the Sonoran Desert. It lies in southwestern Arizona, in southeastern California, and in parts of Mexico. This desert covers about 120,000 square miles.

Because it is farther south, the Sonoran Desert has the highest average temperature of the U.S. deserts. Across large portions of the desert, temperatures may rise above 120°F during the day. However, the nights and winter months are mild. Temperatures seldom drop below freezing.

Rainfall in the Sonoran Desert creates a natural habitat for animals, like the common Mexican tree frog.

Though it may seem unusual, the Sonoran Desert is also one of the wettest deserts in North America. Rain falls in both the winter and summer, but the high temperatures cause most of the water to evaporate. The average rainfall is between three and sixteen inches per year. Rainbows are common during the short, heavy summer rains.

Snow can be found at any time of the year at higher elevations in the Great Basin Desert.

The Great Basin Desert

North of the Mojave Desert is the Great Basin Desert. It is the largest desert in the United States, covering about 190,000 square miles. Its precipitation is between seven and twelve inches per year.

This desert is also known as a "cold desert" because most of its precipitation is in the form of snow, not rain. The cold is a result of its high elevation. Most areas of the desert are between 4,000 and 6,500 feet above sea level. The desert's highest peaks are more than 13,000 feet above sea level. In those high places, snow falls often, even in the summer.

255

CHAPTER 5

Other Deserts Around the World

Polar Deserts

More than 24 large deserts can be found around the world. The largest by far are the Antarctic and the Arctic Deserts, each covering more than 5 million square miles. These polar deserts are covered by snow, ice, glaciers, rocks, and tundra.

The air surrounding Antarctica and the Arctic is so cold that very little precipitation falls each year.

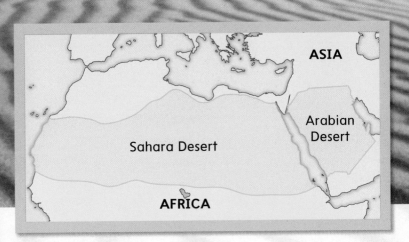

ASIA

Arabian Desert

Sahara Desert

AFRICA

The Sahara Desert

The third-largest desert in the world spreads across northern Africa: the Sahara Desert. It covers more than 3 million square miles. This desert is famous for its sand dunes—some over 500 feet tall! But they cover only a small part of the desert. Most of the Sahara Desert is made of rocky plateaus.

The Sahara Desert is one of the most severe places in the world. Almost no rain will fall for several years in some areas. Summer temperatures are often above 100°F during the day. After the sun sets, the temperature may fall more than 40 degrees. Strong, hot winds create sand storms and "dust devils."

The light and sand can play tricks on your eyes! What might look like a pool of water in the distance is only a mirage.

The Arabian Desert

The Arabian Desert lies in the Middle East. It stretches over the Arabian Peninsula for about 900,000 square miles. Along the coast, the air becomes humid. This causes fog at night and early morning. The desert interior is hot and dry, reaching nearly 130°F.

Sand dunes change shape as the hot wind blows over them. The bright sunlight and smooth sandy surface can create a mirage.

Two More Huge Deserts: The Gobi and the Patagonian

At 500,000 square miles, the Gobi Desert covers parts of northern Asia. This desert is caused by a rain shadow from the Himalaya Mountains. Besides sandy soil and rocks, the Gobi Desert also has dry grasslands, called steppes.

Like the Great Basin Desert, the Gobi is a cold desert. Winter temperatures may fall to 40°F below zero. Summer heat reaches 100°F.

The Patagonian Desert is a cold desert, too. Its gravel plains and plateaus stretch down the long Argentina coast in South America. The Andes Mountains block moisture from the Pacific Ocean. Winter weather occurs seven months of the year. Strong winds blow dust across the continent and into the Atlantic Ocean.

Deserts are found in every continent on Earth. Like other landforms, deserts are diverse. What desert would you like to explore someday?

Dry grasslands called steppes cover parts of the Gobi Desert.

You will answer the comprehension questions on these pages as a class.

Text Connections

1. Does the title "Hot Enough to Fry an Egg" describe all the deserts in this text? Why or why not?

2. How are deserts the same around the world? How are they different? Find evidence in the text to support your answer.

3. On page 254, why does the author say "it may seem unusual" that the Sonoran Desert is one of the wettest deserts in North America?

4. What is extreme about the weather in a desert? How does it compare to the extreme weather described in "Storm Chasers"?

Did You Know?

The hottest temperature ever recorded was at Death Valley in the Mojave Desert. On July 10, 1913, it reached 134 degrees Fahrenheit. No wonder that place in California is called Furnace Creek!

Look Closer

Keys to Comprehension

1. How does the Mojave "rain shadow" form?

Writer's Craft

2. What is *precipitation* and what does it have to do with deserts?

3. How do the descriptions and images of the various deserts compare to your own thoughts of what a desert is like?

Concept Development

4. How do the maps add to the information about deserts in the text?

5. The first three chapters discuss the Mojave Desert, but Chapter 4 and Chapter 5 do not. How are those last two chapters connected to the earlier ones?

Write

Make a list of supplies you would need if you were traveling through one of the deserts you have read about. Make sure you take into account the weather conditions of whichever desert you choose.

Read this story. Then discuss it with your class.

Vocabulary Words

- **Antarctic**
- **continent**
- **elevation**
- **evaporate**
- **extinct**
- **mirage**
- **plateaus**
- **polar**
- **sandwiched**
- **severe**
- **tundra**
- **vapor**

A Polar Adventure

Hakeem could barely hear his own thoughts over the sound of the helicopter dropping him off on the Antarctic continent. He was sandwiched in his seat between his mom and dad, who are scientists. His parents had been sent to research the polar tundra. Hakeem came along, hoping to see a few wild animals that did not live back in the United States.

The helicopter dropped them off on a plateau, which is an elevated flat area of land. It was very high off the ground. When Hakeem stepped out of the helicopter, he thought he saw a huge wooly mammoth in the distance! But it was only a mirage. He remembered that the wooly mammoth is extinct. When he looked again, he saw only snow and ice.

Hakeem's parents took out an instrument to measure the temperature. It was -45 degrees. But that is a relatively warm day for Antarctica. During the summer months, temperatures can get as low as -100 degrees! In such severely cold temperatures, even water vapor will freeze instantly. Since much of the water is frozen, evaporation happens very slowly.

Hakeem and his parents walked around the plateau. His parents picked up pieces of ice to examine. Hakeem began to realize he would not see too many wild animals.

"Why is it so cold here?" Hakeem asked them.

"There are a couple of reasons," his mom replied. "First, Antarctica is very high above sea level. The higher up the land is, the colder it is. Also, there are fewer clouds here to trap the heat. The heat is reflected back up into the sky."

Hakeem bundled up his thick coat and shivered. *No wonder so few animals live here!* he thought.

Concept Vocabulary

Think about the word *climate*. How would you describe the climate of your community?

Extend Vocabulary

Copy the word web into your Writer's Notebook. Fill it in with words related to *extinct*, including antonyms, synonyms, and related words.

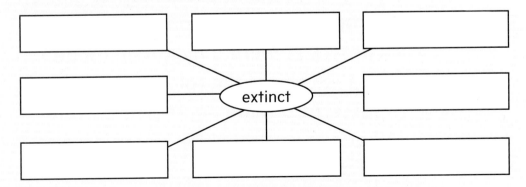

Read this Science Connection. You will answer the questions as a class.

Text Feature

An **abbreviation** is a shortened form of a word.

Dry Dry Dry

Deserts are located on every continent on Earth. Deserts generally get less than 25 centimeters (cm), or about 10 inches, of rain a year. It does not matter if it has severe heat or is made of frozen tundra. Some deserts might actually get more than 25 cm of precipitation in any one year. The Sonoran Desert can get up to 40 cm of rain a year. On the other hand, rain or snow has never been recorded at the Atacama Desert in northern Chile.

There are 24 really large deserts in the world. You read about nine of them in "Hot Enough to Fry an Egg." Using print or digital resources, find the Great Victoria Desert, the Kalahari Desert, and the Chihuahuan Desert on a map or globe. List them in a chart. Then record the following information about them: Size, Continent, and Type (hot, cool, cold).

Once you have this information, compare the deserts. Use a map or globe to find out additional information about each desert. Is there a mountain range nearby that blocks the rain? How far is each desert from the equator?

What can you conclude about deserts around the world?

1. If the Sonoran Desert can get up to 40 cm of rain in a year, why is it still considered a desert?

2. Why do you think the first use of the abbreviation "cm" is in parentheses? How is it used after that?

3. Pick one of the three additional deserts you researched and describe its climate.

 Go Digital

Search for a list of the largest deserts you have not learned about yet. Then search for desert types or names of deserts to gather information.

"Einstein, look at this. It's really scary."

Einstein Anderson's best friend, Paloma Fuentes, handed him her phone. He pushed his glasses back on his nose and looked at the screen. It was a video of ocean waves breaking over a house near the seashore. He nodded grimly.

"Yeah, that's pretty bad," he said, handing the phone back.

"I wonder if this Dr. Raynes really has invented something that can stop hurricanes," Paloma said. "Is it possible?"

"I guess that's what we're going to find out," Einstein replied. "If he could, it would be incredible. It would save thousands of lives and billions of dollars."

It was a Tuesday evening in mid-April and they were sitting in the middle of Sparta High School's auditorium. All around them people were filing in, looking for seats. But Einstein and Paloma were the only sixth graders there.

Some of the adults looked pretty worried. A hurricane had recently torn through the town of Sparta, blowing over trees, knocking down power lines, and causing a lot of damage. Luckily no one had been hurt, but it had been very scary.

Now, someone named Dr. Raynes had called an emergency town meeting at the high school. He said he had a plan for dealing with future hurricanes. He'd even taken out an ad in the *Sparta Tribune* and placed notices on local blogs. Einstein's mother, Emily Anderson, was an editor and reporter for the *Tribune*. She decided to attend the meeting to see what Dr. Raynes had to say and she invited Einstein along, just in case she needed a science expert.

Anyone who knew Einstein wouldn't have been surprised that his mother sometimes turned to him for help with science facts. Even though he was only twelve, Einstein Anderson was famous in the town of Sparta for his amazing knowledge of science and for the way he used science to solve mysteries, both big and small. That's how he got the nickname, Einstein, after the greatest scientific genius of the twentieth century. His real name was Adam, but no one called him that anymore, not even his parents.

Albert Einstein was a world-famous thinker who came up with the equation $E = mc^2$. That simple equation helped lead to atomic energy and a new understanding of the universe. Einstein Anderson, however, was just an average-looking twelve-year-old kid with light brown hair and glasses that seemed too big for his face.

He and Paloma had been friends for a few years. They both went to Sparta Middle School. Paloma was the only person he'd met, or at least the only person his age, who loved science as much as he did—or maybe more. Paloma was taller than Einstein and she always wore her straight black hair in a ponytail, just like she always wore her red canvas high-top sneakers.

Emily Anderson turned to her son. "Einstein, I spoke with Dr. Raynes briefly. He says he has a way to stop hurricanes. I don't understand how anyone could claim to be able to stop hurricanes," she said. "I mean, some of these storms are hundreds of miles across. How could you stop that?"

"Well, some researchers have talked about it," Einstein told her. "Especially since hurricanes seem to be getting bigger and bigger. The way you would stop a hurricane is to do something about heat."

"Heat?" his mom asked.

"Yes," Paloma explained, picking up where Einstein left off. "Hurricanes form over the ocean in the tropics, where the water is warmed by the sun. The air over the ocean heats up and, as you know, hot air rises."

"Yes, I did know that," Emily Anderson said with a smile. She was also used to having Paloma explain things to her.

"Well," Paloma continued, sounding a little bit like a professor, "the more heat in the ocean, the more the hot air rises. But other, cooler air has to come in to replace the hot air. Then that air heats up, and it rises. And if that keeps happening, you get a whirlpool of air rushing in—that's a hurricane."

"Well, after hearing that, I certainly hope this Dr. Raynes has a solution," Mrs. Anderson said.

"Did you ask him what he's a doctor of?" Einstein said to his mom.

"I did," Emily Anderson replied with a frown. "He avoided the question, but I plan to ask him again tonight."

"All this talk about hurricanes reminds me of something," Einstein began, but both Paloma and his mom quickly interrupted him.

"No jokes, Einstein," Paloma warned.

"Einstein, must you?" his mother asked.

But when it came to corny jokes, Einstein Anderson could not be stopped.

"How does a hurricane see where it's going?" he said with a chuckle.

"That's easy, Einstein," Paloma replied. "With its eye!" Even though Paloma knew the punch line, Einstein laughed anyway.

Just then, the crowd hushed as a tall, good-looking young man dressed in jeans and a black turtleneck sweater walked out onto the stage. He had thick, wavy black hair and a big, confident smile. He grabbed the microphone like a pop singer and began talking quickly and excitedly.

"Hurricanes!" he cried. "For centuries mankind has wondered how the destructive force of these terrible storms can be stopped. Now, for the first time we have an answer. My name is Dr. Phillip Raynes, and that's what I'm going to talk about tonight."

There was a rumble from the audience as everyone reacted to this news. But the audience quickly quieted down and listened, as Dr. Raynes paced back and forth across the stage. While he talked, photographs of hurricanes and their damage were projected on the screen behind him. With each image of destruction, he became more and more excited.

Finally, he paused, and then said in a dramatic voice, "As you know, the secret to the strength of hurricanes is the heat from the ocean!" Einstein and Paloma nodded in agreement. "That's also their weakness. We can stop hurricanes if we can cool down the water in the ocean."

"Yeah, but how are you going to do that?" Paloma muttered.

As if he had heard her, Dr. Raynes replied, "I know you're asking, 'How are we going to do that?' The answer is—with icebergs!"

The crowd reacted with a hum of talk as a video started playing on the screen behind him. It was an animated view of a giant iceberg being towed across the ocean into a hurricane. Dr. Raynes went on for a few more minutes. The more he talked, the more the audience rumbled. It seemed to Einstein that some people were excited about the idea of stopping hurricanes. But others were angry that they had come out to hear this crazy idea.

On stage, Raynes gave his closing pitch.

"Now, usually I would write a proposal for a research grant from the government," he said with a big, knowing smile. "But we all know how slow the government is."

Several people in the audience nodded and laughed.

Dr. Raynes nodded and continued. "That's why I've decided to build my hurricane halting machine privately—by forming my own company, Hurri-Can't, Incorporated. And you, lucky enough to be here today, can be among the first investors!"

Some people applauded, but others shook their heads. When things quieted down, Dr. Raynes looked out over the audience.

"Now, I'm sure some of you have questions," he said. "Who will be first?"

Almost before the words were out of his mouth, Paloma raised her hand. Dr. Raynes's face lit up with a big grin.

"Yes, young woman," he said with amusement. "What's your question?"

Paloma stood up.

"I'm Paloma Fuentes," she said. "And I don't see how you're going to get an iceberg big enough to cool off the ocean." Paloma wasn't very big, but her voice carried everywhere in the auditorium.

"Well, it's rather complicated, I'm afraid," Raynes replied. "Let's just say I don't need a really giant iceberg. You see, hurricanes are formed from high-pressure systems. The high pressure pushes the air outward in all directions. So the iceberg doesn't have to cool off the whole ocean, just disrupt the high-pressure air pattern. Did you understand that?"

"No," Paloma said with an angry frown.

"You could look at my website," Dr. Raynes said, very kindly. "It has a whole kids section that explains everything. Uh, next question?"

As Paloma sat down, she muttered, "I didn't understand it because it doesn't make any sense."

Now Einstein had his hand up. On the stage, Dr. Raynes laughed.

"My goodness," he said. "We have another young questioner. I'm glad that young people are so concerned about the environment. And what's your name, young man?"

Einstein stood up.

"Einstein Anderson," he answered, but his voice squeaked as he said it. A few people laughed. Dr. Raynes looked very serious.

"Einstein? Really?" he said. "Ladies and gentlemen, it seems we have a genius in the audience. Well, Einstein, what's your question? Do you also want proof that my machine will work?"

"Einstein is my nickname," Einstein said, very calmly. "And I don't have a question. I also have no idea if your machine will work, though I doubt it. But I can prove that you don't know anything about hurricanes."

Can you solve the mystery? How can Einstein prove Dr. Raynes doesn't understand hurricanes?

The smile on Dr. Raynes's face got even bigger.

"Really, *Mr. Einstein*?" he said mockingly. "How will you prove that?"

Einstein pushed the glasses up his nose. "I can prove it because what you said about hurricanes is exactly backwards," he replied.

"You said that hurricanes are caused by high pressure systems. That's wrong. As the hot air rises at the center of a hurricane, it creates a big drop in air pressure. A hurricane is a large area of very *low* pressure, not *high* pressure at all. The low pressure is what causes the powerful winds to blow in a spiral toward the center."

As Einstein finished, Dr. Raynes's broad face slowly turned bright pink. For a moment, he was speechless.

"Young man, I'm… I'm sure you mean well," he sputtered. "But I think I know better than… "

"He's right!" someone shouted from the other side of the hall.

"Of course, I'm right," Raynes replied with a huff.

A man stood up near the back of the auditorium. He held up a smartphone.

"Not you!" he cried, then he pointed to Einstein. "Him! The kid is right! I just looked it up online."

The room erupted, with everyone talking at once. On either side, Einstein could see people taking out their phones and checking for themselves.

Paloma stood up and, in a clear voice that carried over the din, she shouted, "Of course he's right! That's why they call him *Einstein*!"

Raynes looked from left to right. Some folks in the audience had even started booing him. Without another word, he hurried from the stage.

"Well, this is going to be an interesting article," Mrs. Anderson said, as they left the auditorium. "Thanks to you, *Einstein*."

"I wonder what that guy was a doctor of," Paloma said. "Probably of fakeology."

"Hey, that reminds me!" Einstein said with a laugh.

Paloma groaned, "Oh, no, here it comes!"

But Einstein's mother nodded, "Go ahead Einstein, you earned it."

"Do you know why the house needed to see a doctor?" he asked. Then before anyone could answer, he burst out with, "Because it had window pains!"

From: Einstein Anderson

To: Science Geeks

Experiment: How to Build Your Own Barometer

My friend Paloma knew that Dr. Raynes was a fake the minute he said hurricanes were caused by wind circulating around an area of *high* pressure, because she knew that the centers of hurricanes are areas with very *low* pressure. But what's this air-pressure thing all about? How do changes in air pressure affect our weather? And how do meteorologists (that's people who study the weather—like the weatherperson on TV) measure air pressure?

Let's build our own barometer to measure air pressure and start to predict the weather!

Here is what you need:

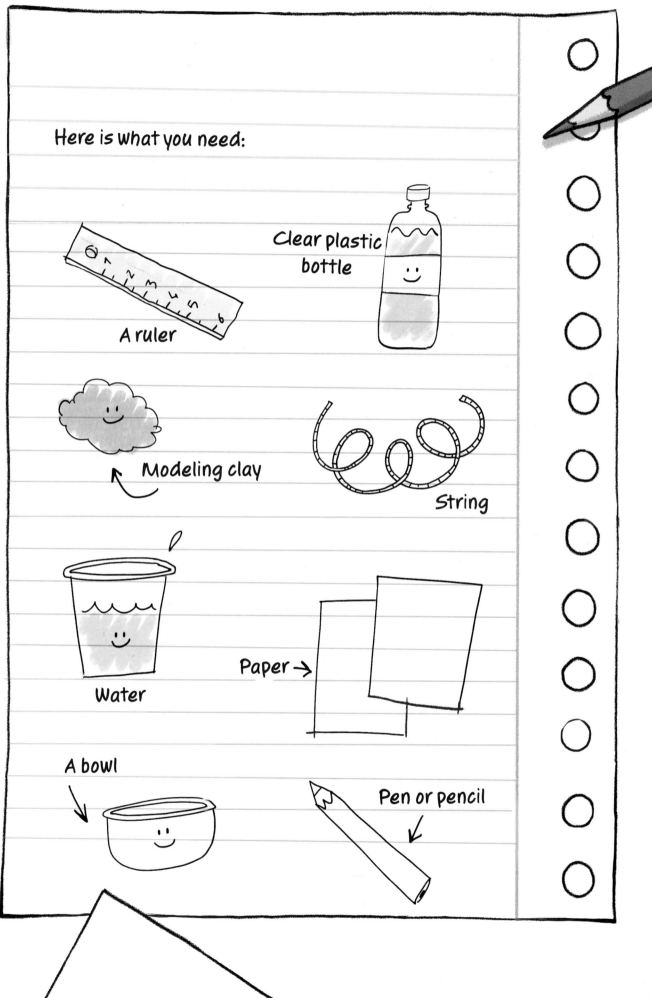

A ruler

Clear plastic bottle

Modeling clay

String

Water

Paper →

A bowl

Pen or pencil

Put a lump of clay in the bottom of the bowl and stick the ruler into it so it stands up straight. Pour enough water into the bowl to fill it about 1/3 full. Then fill the clear bottle about 3/4 full of water. Put your hand over the top to keep the water from running out and turn it over, upside down, into the bowl. Once the top of the bottle is under water, you can take your hand away and the water won't run out. Use your string to tie the bottle to the ruler.

Cut out a strip of paper 4 inches long and mark lines on it every 1/4 inch. Use a dark line to mark the middle of the strip. Tape or glue this to the water bottle so that the dark line matches the level of water in the bottle.

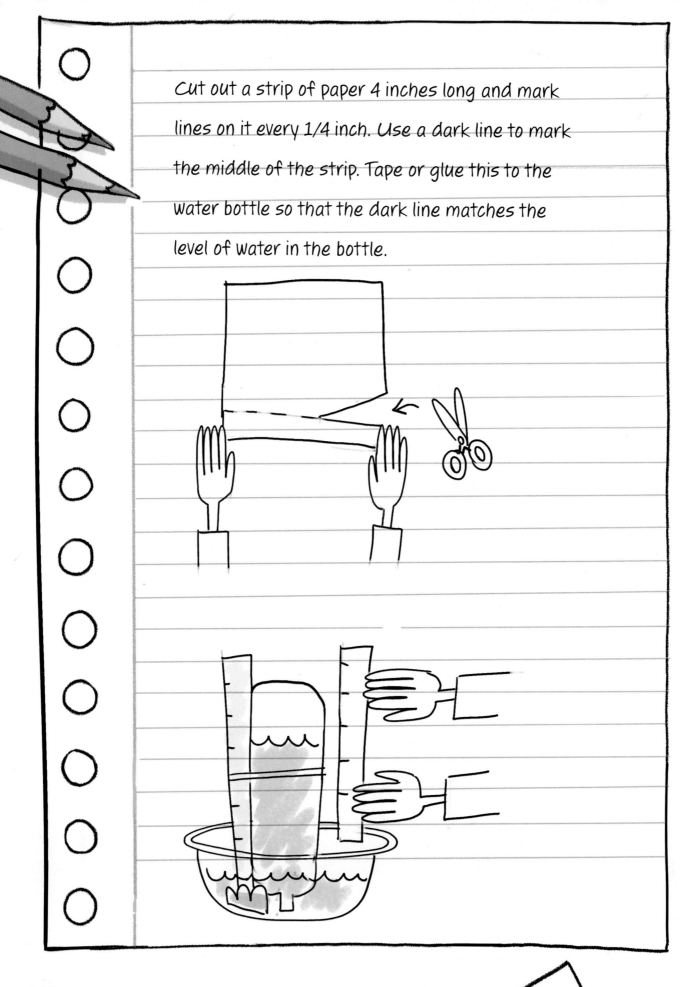

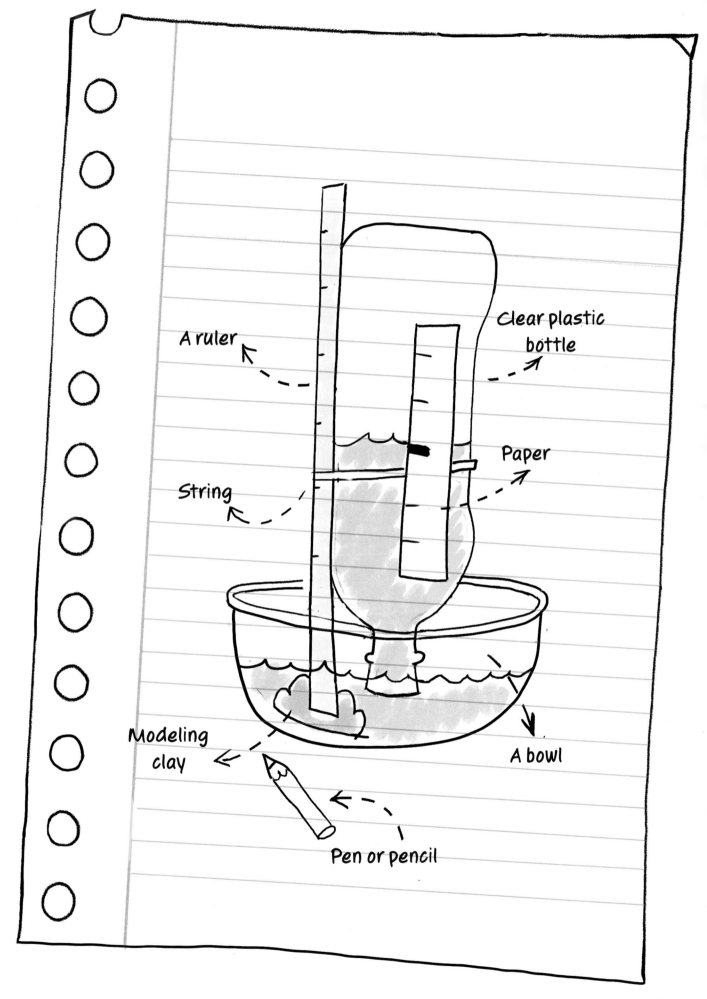

That's it! You have a water barometer. When the air pressure rises, it will press down with more force on the water in the bowl and force water up into the bottle. You will see that the water level goes up to a higher pressure line. When the air pressure falls, it will press with less force on the water in the bowl and some of the water in the bottle will flow out into the bowl. On a low pressure day, the water line in the bottle will fall below the dark line on your paper.

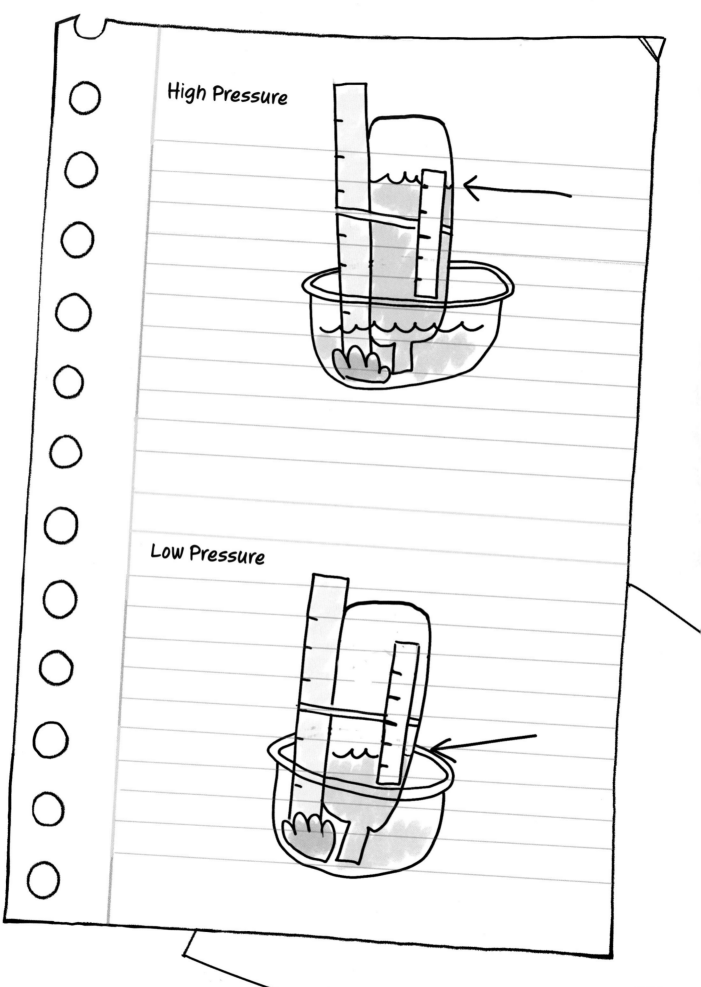

High Pressure

Low Pressure

301

Look up your local weather online or on TV and keep track of the air pressure, or barometric pressure, for a few days. Your water barometer won't be as accurate as the ones the weather service uses, but you should see the water level change up and down along with the weather report. In general, high pressure goes with sunshine and good weather, while low pressure usually means cloudy or rainy weather. Did you notice that while you kept track of the air pressure with your water barometer?

So now, what does air pressure have to do with the weather? I'm glad you asked.

Let's keep in mind a few things:

1 Hot air rises.

2 Higher air pressure creates greater force and pushes things around.

3 Low pressure does not "pull" objects or particles, but when hot air rises it creates a vacuum, which heavier, colder air flows in to fill. The difference in barometric pressure between high pressure and low pressure areas causes wind – and hurricanes.

As Paloma said, hurricanes form in the late summer when the water temperatures in the ocean rise above 80° Fahrenheit (26.6° Celsius). The warm water heats the air and makes water vapor rise into the atmosphere, where it cools and forms clouds. Colder air, in turn, comes in below and is warmed by the water until it rises. All this movement creates a low pressure area, ripe for conversion to a serious storm.

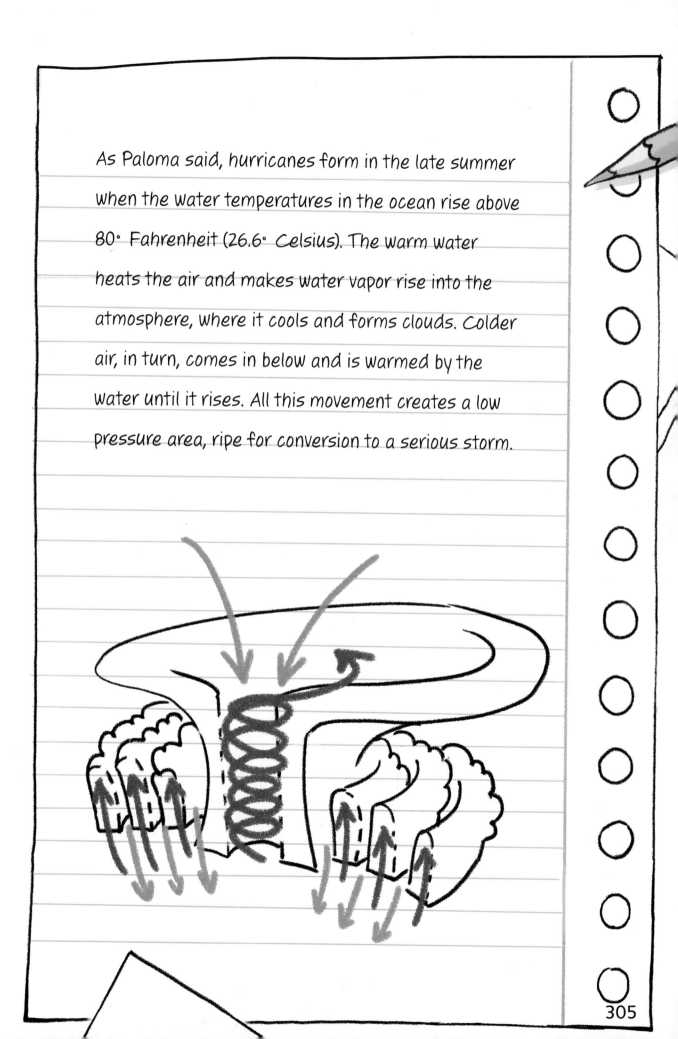

Text Connections

1. How do hurricanes form?

2. Why do Einstein and Paloma go to the town meeting? What might have happened later in the story if they did not go?

3. Use what you read in "Tornadoes!" and the experiment section of this story to describe the similarities and differences between a tornado and a hurricane.

4. In "Get the Facts" you learn that the school building was built to withstand storm damage. It had a wind-resistant roof and shatter-resistant glass. How do those solutions compare to the solution Dr. Raynes proposes for hurricanes?

Did You Know?

In the Northern Hemisphere, hurricanes always spin counterclockwise. In the Southern Hemisphere, they always spin clockwise. This is caused by the rotation of Earth and one of the fundamental principles of physics known as *inertia*.

Look Closer

Keys to Comprehension

1. What is the central message of the story? How is this conveyed through Einstein proving Dr. Raynes is a fake?

2. How do the students in this story compare to the students in "Get the Facts"?

Writer's Craft

3. What does it mean that "the room erupted" after Einstein challenged Dr. Raynes?

4. Why do you think the author stops the story on page 267 to ask the reader to try to solve the mystery?

Concept Development

5. How do the illustrations that accompany Einstein's barometer experiment help you understand it? Is there any information in the illustrations that is not in the written instructions?

Write
What kind of weather hazards would you like to prevent? Why?

Read this Science Connection.
You will answer the questions as a class.

Text Feature

Diagrams are drawings. They show the arrangement or parts of something.

Beating the Weather

In "Einstein Anderson and the Hurricane Hoax" Professor Raynes claimed that he had found a way to stop hurricanes from happening. He sounded confident, like he knew what he was talking about, but as Einstein proved, he did not.

In the story, the solution was a hoax. It was based on wrong information and faulty thinking. But some of the best solutions have come from what at first seemed like wacky ideas. Science is all about coming up with ideas and testing them and retesting them to make sure the results are the same.

Think of weather problems in your area. Is heat a problem? Is cold? Is it too wet or too dry? Do you experience hurricanes, blizzards, thunderstorms, or tornadoes? Think of ideas that people have had to deal with the weather. Some houses may be up on stilts in case of flooding. Homes in the tropics may be painted light colors to reflect the sun. Some may not have basements because of moisture. Some windows might be made of plastic instead of glass so they will not break in a storm. Some buildings may be designed to keep out the heat or the cold.

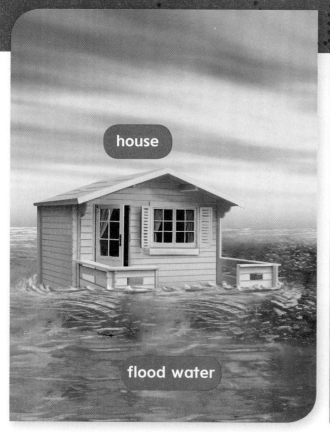

1. Look at the diagram above. How does this design solution reduce the impact of a flood? What are the drawbacks of this design?

2. Why do scientists need to test their ideas? What would happen if they did not test them?

3. What weather-related problems does your community face? What solutions are already in place?

 Go Digital

Search for weather-related problems and current solutions for those problems. Think of additional solutions to the problems.

BIG Idea

How can we learn from our past?

Theme Connections

How has transportation changed over time?

Background Builder Video
connected.mcgraw-hill.com

Genre Historical Fiction

Essential Questions

How did immigrants help build the country?
How would you feel if you had to immigrate
to an unfamiliar place?

A New Life for Mei

by Judy Kentor Schmauss
illustrated by Ron Mezellan

"Here at last, Mei," Hong said to his wife. "California! We are finally here!"

Mei and Hong left China in 1867 to start a new life. Hong's uncle had come to America in 1849, looking for gold. Although he was very poor, he sent letters home detailing his travels in America. He was not one of the lucky few to strike it rich, but he enjoyed his adventures in the new land. Due to his letters, Hong and Mei decided to try their own luck in San Francisco.

Mei stared at the sea of unfamiliar faces around them as their boat neared the port.

Hong and Mei soon settled in the Chinatown community, home to numerous Chinese immigrants just like them. Hong got a job on the Transcontinental Railroad. The railroad was being built to link the East and West Coasts of the United States together. Hong was one of the thousands of Chinese men who would work to complete the western side of the railroad.

Hong was a good worker. It was a hard job, but he was proud to work on such an important project. And they needed the money. However, Hong would have to leave Mei by herself in order to work many miles from home. He would be gone until the railroad was complete.

Mei was apprehensive about being alone in the city. The people of Chinatown worked together to support each other, but there were few jobs, and Mei spoke less English than Hong. She did not know how she would manage.

After Hong left, Mei eventually found work.
In China, she had always enjoyed helping her
parents prepare family meals. In San Francisco,
she found a job working as an assistant to Mrs.
Hatch, the manager of the kitchen at one of the
city's nicest hotels.

Mei proved herself to be a valuable employee.
Mrs. Hatch was temperamental and untrusting,
but over time, she gave Mei more and more
responsibilities. The restaurant was always busy,
but Mei thought that was because it was located
in a good spot, rather than because it had good
food. Even so, Mrs. Hatch complained all the time.
"I have so much work!" Mrs. Hatch whined. *What
work?* Mei thought as she worked her own fingers
to the bone.

Days stretched together. Then weeks and months passed. Mei had not heard from Hong for a long time. She heard others in her community discuss the dangers of working on the railroad. She heard stories about Chinese workers who were treated badly by other workers. She began to worry.

One Thursday evening, Mrs. Hatch had a special announcement to make.

"I just found out that Mr. James Fischer is coming to the hotel on Saturday night. He is a very wealthy businessman from the East. He's meeting a group of important men that night, so nothing must go wrong!" Mei nodded.

Mrs. Hatch turned to leave. In her rush, she never saw the delivery man who was coming through the door. She crashed right into the poor man, sending fruits and vegetables flying. Mei let out a gasp as Mrs. Hatch toppled over and landed awkwardly on her arm.

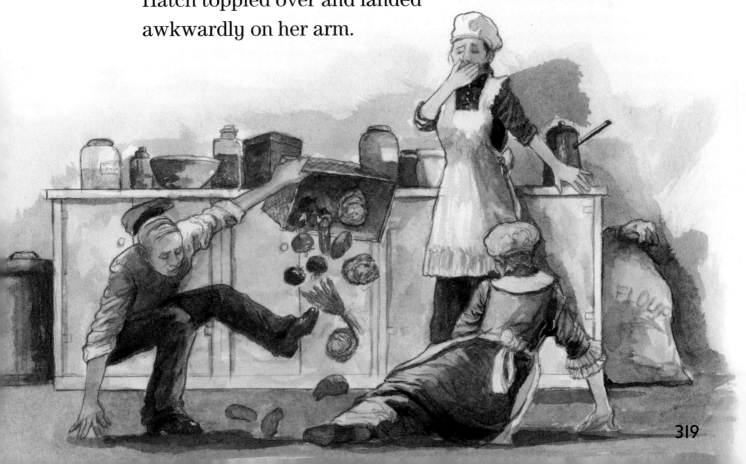

The next morning, the hotel's owner told Mei, "I'm sorry to say that Mrs. Hatch fractured her arm and won't be coming back to work until it heals. You will have to take over the kitchen until she comes back. Don't forget though, that Mr. Fischer will be here tomorrow night! You will need to accommodate his group. I trust you with this responsibility," he said, firmly but gently. "Please don't let me down."

Mei worked hard for the next two days. The meal she served Mr. Fischer and his business partners was quickly devoured. As the evening ended, it was clear that everything went off without a hitch. Mr. Fischer was so impressed that he came back every night for a week. Each time, he brought more and more guests. Mei quickly realized she would need more help.

The next day, Mei brought some of her friends from Chinatown to the hotel. Like Mei, their husbands were working on the railroad, far from home. After seeing Mei in action, the hotel owner was more than happy to hire them. Led by Mei, they planned meals and prepared wonderful dishes. Every skill they had learned in China was coming into play. Mr. Fischer was so impressed that he asked to meet Mei. He thanked her for the delicious food and promised to tell all of his friends about her wonderful food. Mei was honored to meet such an important man. After their meeting, the restaurant was packed every night.

Mei loved what she was doing. She poured her heart into making everything run smoothly. She was always looking for new dishes to prepare. As a result, the restaurant became even more popular.

Mrs. Hatch returned six weeks after her fall. When she returned to the kitchen, she saw that it had been completely reorganized. She looked at the menu and saw dishes that she did not recognize. Mrs. Hatch grew very angry.

She bellowed at Mei, "Why have you changed the menu? I have taught you exactly how to run a proper kitchen, but you insisted on doing it your own way. This is my kitchen, and I will not have anyone changing it without my approval! All of you, get out and don't come back!" Mei sighed, put her apron on the table, and walked out with her friends.

Things did not go well that night at the restaurant. Orders were mixed up, the service was terrible, and customers complained. Mrs. Hatch blamed Mei every time something went wrong. Not one to ever admit she was wrong, Mrs. Hatch was confident that things would be just fine the next day. She would go out and hire local women to take the place of Mei and her friends. "I'll show them!" Mrs. Hatch declared.

A week later, Mr. Fischer returned to the restaurant and ordered his favorite dish. He was quite surprised when it tasted nothing like what he had been expecting. Sending for the cook, he was shocked to see Mrs. Hatch come out of the kitchen instead of Mei.

"I got rid of her," Mrs. Hatch said to Mr. Fischer. "I couldn't count on her to run the kitchen properly. Now I'll show you just how this place *should* be run."

"No, I will show *you*." Mr. Fischer said politely, "I have just purchased this hotel. *You*, madam, no longer work here."

Meanwhile, Mei had begun looking for a new job, without much success. She was living on the money she had saved while working and it wouldn't last long. Her friends in the community helped her move to an apartment, but it was small and off a dark alley. It was all she could afford but they were happy to help.

Mei also worried because she had not heard from Hong in months. Was this to be her fate in the United States?

One sunny day, Mei found herself studying a map at the general store. She was thinking that it might be time to see what kind of work she could find elsewhere in California. Suddenly she heard her name called. It was Mr. Fischer! She had not seen him in weeks.

When Mr. Fischer found out why Mei was looking at a map of California, he asked her to reconsider. "Please, gather your friends and meet me outside the hotel," he said politely. Mei had a feeling that things were about to change for the better.

In the spring of 1869, just a few months after Mei and Mr. Fischer met at the store, the last tie of the Transcontinental Railroad was fastened. The conditions for the workers had been difficult. Mei could not imagine what Hong must have lived through. *If he lived at all,* she thought to herself. There had still been no word from Hong. And Mei had so much news to share with him! She was now the manager and head chef of the hotel restaurant.

Where was Hong? Why hadn't he come back yet? The railroad was finished, and Mei was beginning to lose hope. But Hong had returned! He simply did not know where Mei was. Some of the neighbors told him where she was working.

Once he arrived at the hotel, one of her friends took him to Mei's office. There was so much excitement that Mr. Fischer came to see what was happening. Mr. Fischer shook Hong's hand and told him how important Mei was. Hong agreed.

You will answer the comprehension questions on these pages as a class.

Text Connections

1. Why do Mei and Hong come to the United States?

2. What makes Mei worry? What makes Mei happy?

3. Why do you think Mei feels that "things were about to change for the better" after Mr. Fischer approaches her at the general store?

4. Do Mei and Hong find adventures they expected to find in the new land? Use evidence from the text to explain your answer.

Did You Know?

Do you like Chinese food? What we know as Chinese food in America came to the country in the mid-1800s. When Chinese immigrants like Mei and Hong came to California during and after the Gold Rush, some opened restaurants. They served a new kind of food that many people liked.

Look Closer

Keys to Comprehension

1. What does the story say about the importance of hard work?

2. How do you think Mr. Fischer will be as Mei's boss compared to Mrs. Hatch? Why?

Writer's Craft

3. Why do you think the author says that the first meal Mei serves Mr. Fischer and his partners is "quickly devoured"?

4. Why does Mrs. Hatch fire Mei and her friends? Would you have done the same thing?

Concept Development

5. What is the setting for this story? How do the illustrations help clarify that?

Write

Write a story about what happened to Hong during the time he was away from Mei and working on the railroad.

Read the story.
Then discuss it
with your class.

Vocabulary Words

- **accommodate**
- **alley**
- **apprehensive**
- **bellowed**
- **fate**
- **hitch**
- **link**
- **proper**
- **rush**
- **strike**
- **temperamental**
- **tie**

Car Dreams

The old car did not look like much. Its paint was faded. Also, one of its doors did not have a proper handle. A rope tie was all that kept the door from swinging open.

Even so, Dad was excited about the car. "Should we take it for a spin?" he asked. I looked at the car doubtfully and climbed in.

Right away there was a hitch. When Dad tried to start the car, its engine wheezed and then clunked. But Dad patiently tried again, and the temperamental engine started with a bellow. I apprehensively glanced at Dad. I did not know what to expect.

"We'll just take it for a slow drive down the alleys," he chuckled.

The alleys did not make me any less nervous. They were barely wide enough to accommodate one car, and they were bumpy. Once, Dad had to swerve suddenly so as not to strike a pothole. He drove a little more slowly after that. "We don't need to rush, do we?" he asked with a wink.

We rode in silence for a while. Then he said, "This car used to be your grandpa's, you know. We went all over the place in it."

As Dad shared memories of road trips and driving lessons, I finally understood. For him, the car was a link to happy times.

Now, Dad plans to fix up the car like new. "I think fate holds a few more adventures for us," he says, patting its door. I imagine the car all shined up and hope this is true!

Concept Vocabulary

Think about the word *immigrate*. If you could immigrate, where would you go? Why would you go there?

Extend Vocabulary

Copy the word web in your Writer's Notebook. Then fill it in with four words that describe someone who is temperamental.

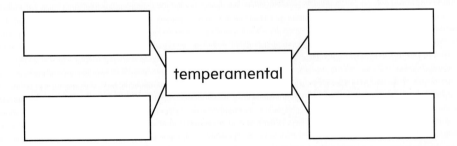

temperamental

Read this Social Studies Connection. You will answer the questions as a class.

Text Feature

A **heading** tells what a section is going to be about.

Earning a Living

New Jobs

Jobs are created when there is more work to be done than there are people to do it. The creation of jobs is tied to the wants and needs of the people.

Wants and Needs

Goods and services can be categorized as either a want or a need. We all *need* food, shelter, and clothing. People may *want* to have better food or a nicer home though. Those are wants, since they are not required for survival.

Supply and Demand

Getting paid for work is a way people earn money. They can spend money to meet their wants and needs. As consumers buy things, the demand is affected. If they buy a lot of one product, the demand goes up and the supply goes down. The producer must make more in order to satisfy the demand.

Our Economy

The relationship between wants, needs, supply, and demand fuels the economy.

People's wants and needs drive production. This creates jobs. If supply cannot keep up with demand, the price will rise. If the price gets too high, fewer people may want the product. That reduces demand. If there is less demand for a product, the people making it could lose their jobs. Meeting wants and needs creates a complicated cycle.

Which of these meals is a want and which is a need?

1. How are the headings before each section helpful?

2. What are some examples of needs? What are examples of wants?

3. What might a company do if their product is in high demand? What if nobody buys the product?

 Go Digital

Search for "types of jobs in schools" to see the different jobs in schools. How does each job meet a need or a want?

Genre Informational Text

Essential Questions
Why would people want to feel like they are part of a community? Is there anything about your community that makes you feel proud?

The Harlem Renaissance

by Matthew Gollub

GIBSON STUDIO PHOTOGRAPHERS

CHIROPODIST

GIBSON STUDIO PHOTOGRAM

A. S. BECK SHOE

EST. 188
WEISBECKER M

RIB LAMB CHOPS
APPLE PIES 12
SELECTED EGGS

Imagine it is the 1920s, and you are in Harlem, a thriving neighborhood of New York City. The night life, the bright lights, even the sidewalks hum with excitement.

The thump-thump of drums and a screaming clarinet draw you into The Savoy nightclub. The Savoy is huge, the size of a city block! The singer Cab Calloway, in his white tuxedo, shakes, swaggers, and chants jazz to the crowd. Across the ballroom, as far as the eye can see, sharply dressed men and women cut loose with the latest dance steps.

Duke Ellington was a legendary jazz pianist and conductor. For years, he performed in Harlem before his fame spread around the world.

In Harlem in the 1920s, exciting jazz was everywhere. New Yorkers from downtown took the A train north. They came for dinner, dancing, and the adventure of something new. "Harlemites," the African American people who lived in Harlem, worked hard, then dressed up and enjoyed going out.

Trumpeter Louis Armstrong pioneered the jazz solo. He became an international star who symbolized tolerance and love.

Harlem's popular nightclubs attracted top jazz players from around the country. A handsome young piano player named Duke Ellington lead bands. The singer Bessie Smith was known as the "Empress of the Blues." And when a young trumpet player named Louis Armstrong began to solo, people fell under the spell of his horn's warmth. No one could deny the genius they heard in these black artists' minds and souls.

The 1920s was called "The Age of Jazz." But the music was only part of a movement. Today we call this proud movement the "Harlem Renaissance." It was when African American poetry and art blossomed. It was when communities of artists sprang up and grew close.

A History of Hardship

During these years, African Americans produced more art than at any time before. Amazingly, they did this while their people faced hardships that today we can only imagine. Even in northern cities, there were "whites only" jazz clubs. The only African Americans allowed in these clubs were the ones performing on stage for white customers.

But in the South, the discrimination was far worse. Jim Crow laws (or "Black Codes") stripped away basic rights. Black people often worked in white people's homes, but their own families were not allowed to live in white neighborhoods. Nor were they welcome in white businesses such as restaurants. Nor were they allowed to pray in white churches. And black children were not allowed to attend white children's schools.

The Great Migration North

Between 1910 and 1930, over one million African Americans left the southern states. This mass exit is known as the "The Great Migration North."

At the time, many worked as "sharecroppers." Sharecroppers were farmers who did not own land. They farmed somebody else's land and paid "rent" with a share of their crops. It was a tough way to scratch out a living to be sure. Things got even tougher when the price of cotton dropped. Then an insect called the boll weevil destroyed cotton crops around the south. Desperate to escape discrimination, and now hunger, more and more African Americans had to leave home.

The northern part of the country was more prosperous than the south. Northern factories needed workers. Southern workers needed to escape grinding poverty. So African Americans flocked to northern cities like New York, Chicago, and Washington, D.C. They came by train, bus, rickety cars, and trucks. They wanted the same things that immigrants hope for today: better jobs, better housing, more freedom, and a better life.

What Brought Them to Harlem

Harlem in the 1920s had it all! It was a prosperous, fashionable, and *black* neighborhood in New York. Sure, it was more expensive to rent an apartment in Harlem. But whether you cut hair in a barbershop or scrubbed floors downtown, it felt good to live in a place that people talked about and enjoyed. As the saying went, "If you're going to be poor anyway, it's better to be poor in Harlem."

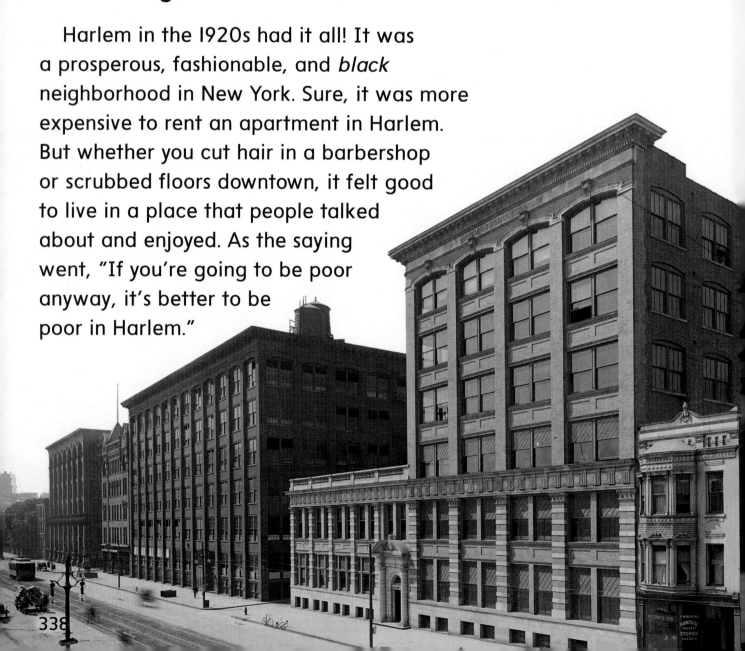

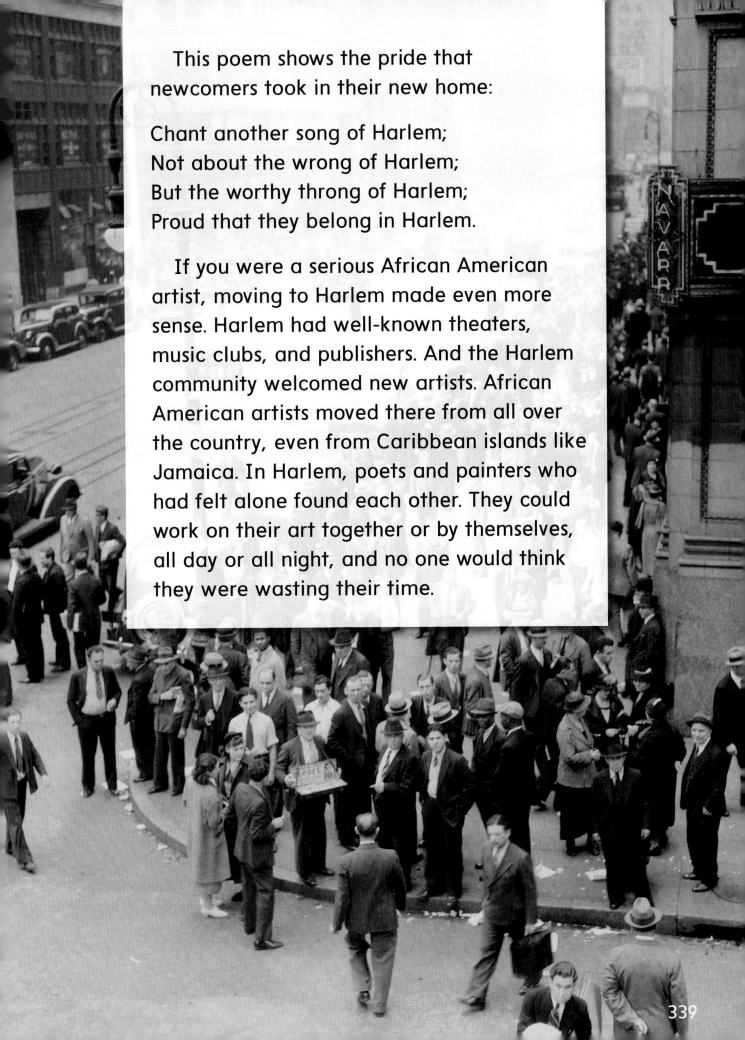

This poem shows the pride that newcomers took in their new home:

Chant another song of Harlem;
Not about the wrong of Harlem;
But the worthy throng of Harlem;
Proud that they belong in Harlem.

If you were a serious African American artist, moving to Harlem made even more sense. Harlem had well-known theaters, music clubs, and publishers. And the Harlem community welcomed new artists. African American artists moved there from all over the country, even from Caribbean islands like Jamaica. In Harlem, poets and painters who had felt alone found each other. They could work on their art together or by themselves, all day or all night, and no one would think they were wasting their time.

Poetry Readings on Any Night

Now imagine you are in Harlem after midnight. Up you climb, three flights of stairs, to arrive in someone's living room. Famous African American poets have gathered with readers eager to share their ideas. There is Countee Cullen wearing a coat and tie. He is a graduate of New York University. He even earned a Master's degree in English from Harvard University. He reads his poem Heritage, a work of soaring verses about Africa. He explains that he has traveled to Africa many times but only, he adds shyly, in his mind's eye.

Another young poet adjusts his bowtie. "My name is Langston Hughes," he begins. Both writers express themselves in crisp English. Their command of words makes it clear that they have studied a great many books. Still, their writing styles are different. Cullen's verse sounds formal, more classical. Hughes writes poems the way ordinary people speak.

After the readings, their editor, Jessie Fauset, claps the loudest. She is the poetry editor of the magazine The Crisis, *and she has helped launch the careers of many Renaissance writers. "Now," she proclaims, "we have a chance to be known to white readers. White readers want to know the truth about black people. And black writers are the most qualified to let that truth be known."*

Talent and Great Works Produced

Talented black artists were ready. They produced poetry, novels, photography, sculpture, theater, dance, and, of course, "the era of jazz." One important book was an anthology, or collection, called *The New Negro*. It contained the works of 34 Harlem writers. It was edited by Alain Locke. Its purpose was to introduce the talents of African American writers who were eager to prove themselves to the world.

The editor and writer Jessie Fauset graduated from Cornell University and studied literature in France. Those she worked with admired her energy and first-rate mind.

Parties, Patrons, and Social Life

In the 1920s, the economy was booming, so well-to-do art lovers spent freely on parties. They would invite friends and celebrities into their homes, including Harlem artists who were suddenly "in fashion." This made it possible for black people and white people to mix in ways that before were not imaginable.

One of the richest and most stylish people in Harlem was A'Lelia Walker. She was six feet tall and wore the finest silks and furs. Her mother had become America's first black female millionaire. She had left A'Lelia a fortune. Langston Hughes called A'Lelia the "Joy Goddess of Harlem" because she loved to help everyone around her enjoy life. In the end she converted her mansion into a club, a place where all types of artists could meet and make friends.

Harlem socialites like A'Lelia Walker threw lavish parties and brought artists together.

Carl Van Vechten, a white writer and "Harlem expert," and his wife would throw lavish parties of their own. He was an example of an arts patron. When he found Harlem writers whose work he admired, he made sure newspapers like *The New York Times* wrote about them. This helped Renaissance writers become known beyond Harlem. He would also regularly lead "tours" to Harlem to introduce his wealthy friends to this community.

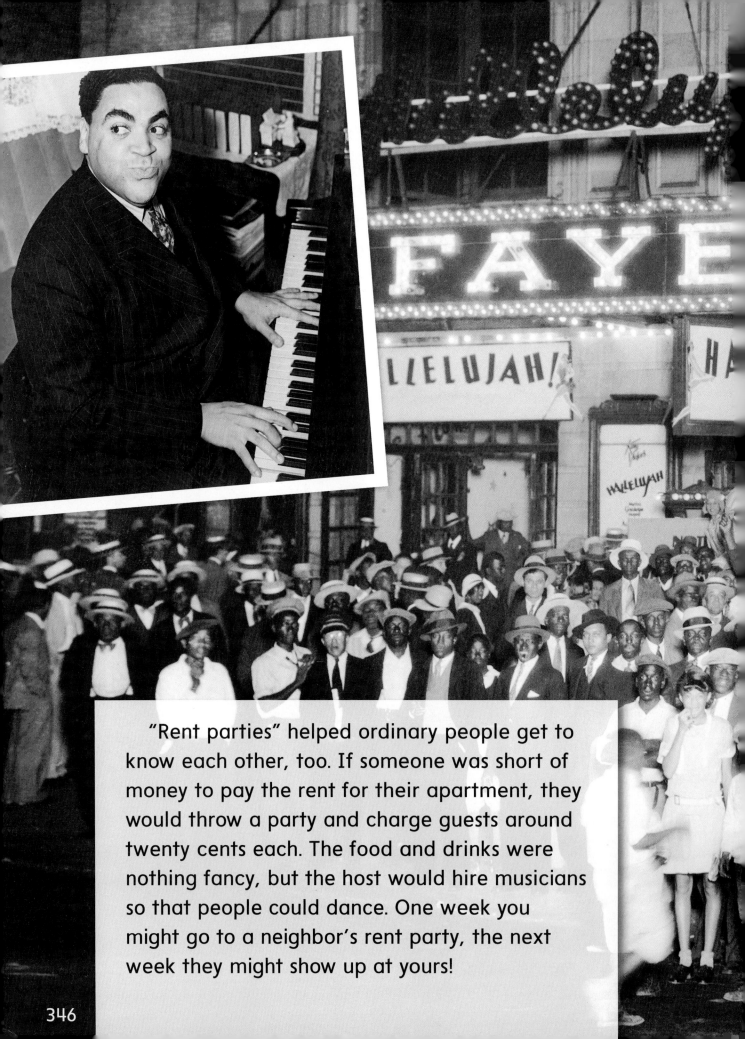

"Rent parties" helped ordinary people get to know each other, too. If someone was short of money to pay the rent for their apartment, they would throw a party and charge guests around twenty cents each. The food and drinks were nothing fancy, but the host would hire musicians so that people could dance. One week you might go to a neighbor's rent party, the next week they might show up at yours!

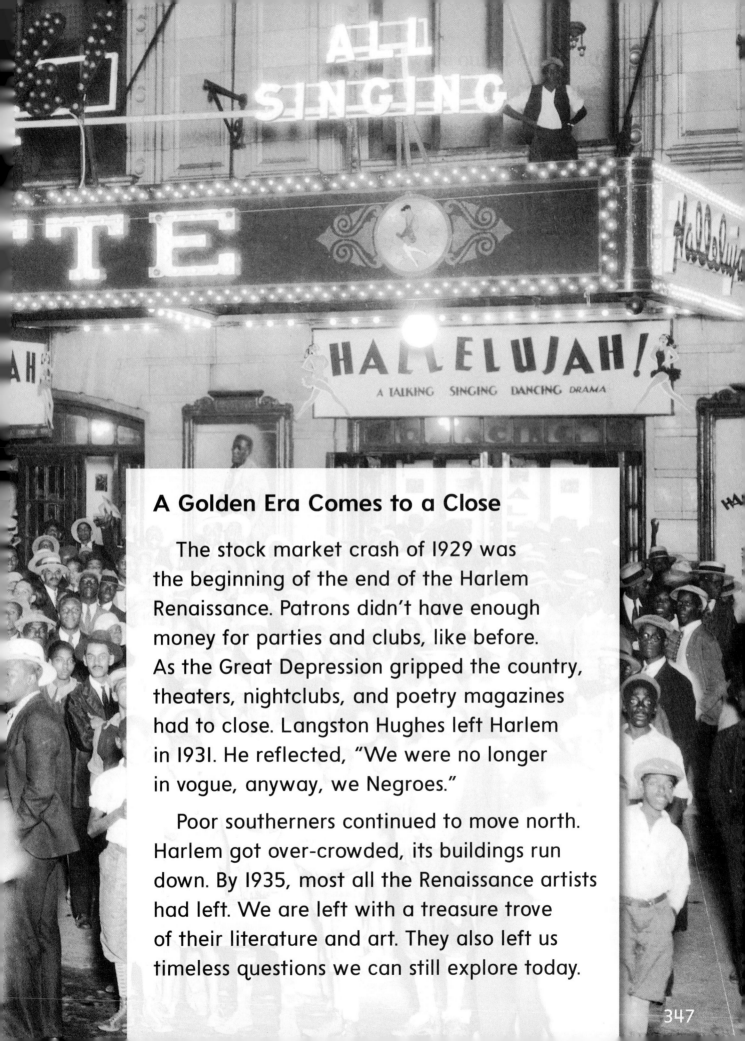

A Golden Era Comes to a Close

The stock market crash of 1929 was the beginning of the end of the Harlem Renaissance. Patrons didn't have enough money for parties and clubs, like before. As the Great Depression gripped the country, theaters, nightclubs, and poetry magazines had to close. Langston Hughes left Harlem in 1931. He reflected, "We were no longer in vogue, anyway, we Negroes."

Poor southerners continued to move north. Harlem got over-crowded, its buildings run down. By 1935, most all the Renaissance artists had left. We are left with a treasure trove of their literature and art. They also left us timeless questions we can still explore today.

The Dream Keeper

by Langston Hughes

Bring me all of your dreams,
You dreamer,
Bring me all your
Heart melodies
That I may wrap them
In a blue cloud-cloth
Away from the too-rough
   fingers
Of the world.

My People

by Langston Hughes

The night is beautiful,
So the faces of my people.

The stars are beautiful,
So the eyes of my people.

Beautiful, also, is the sun.
Beautiful, also, are the souls
  of my people.

Words Like Freedom

by Langston Hughes

There are words like *Freedom*
Sweet and wonderful to say.
On my heartstrings freedom sings
All day everyday.

There are words like *Liberty*
That almost make me cry.
If you had known what I know
You would know why.

You will answer the comprehension questions on these pages as a class.

Text Connections

1. What caused the Harlem Renaissance to begin?

2. Who were three of the famous artists that were part of the Harlem Renaissance and what did they do?

3. What does the word *migration* mean? How can you use context on page 337 to determine its meaning?

4. What does the speaker in "The Dream Keeper" ask the "dreamers" to do with their dreams? Why?

Did You Know?

The Jim Crow laws were put in place after slavery ended. They made it hard for African Americans to vote and made separate schools, libraries, seating, neighborhoods, bathrooms, and other places for black people and white people to use. These laws were overruled by 1965.

Look Closer

Keys to Comprehension

1. Who were A'Lelia Walker and Carl Van Vechten? How did they contribute to the Harlem Renaissance?

2. What caused the Harlem Renaissance to end?

Writer's Craft

3. What does the phrase "blue cloud-cloth" make you think of? Why is it an effective use of language?

4. Why did the author of "The Harlem Renaissance" set some text in italics? What is different about that text?

Concept Development

5. The author states that the Harlem Renaissance was "when African-American poetry and art blossomed." What sections and details does the author provide to support this idea?

Write

Use the Langston Hughes poems as models to write a poem about your dreams.

Read the story. Then discuss it with your class.

Vocabulary Words

- **adventure**
- **cast**
- **dialect**
- **discrimination**
- **fame**
- **international**
- **launch**
- **lavish**
- **pride**
- **prosperous**
- **symbolized**
- **timeless**

A Sweet Partnership

Each summer, my cousin Abi and I entertain ourselves by launching a new sales project. For example, one year we ran a lemonade stand. Another year we sold trail mix from door to door. Abi and I make a good team because each of us has different talents. Abi is famed for his outgoing nature—he's always cast in the role of salesperson. I am known for being creative. So, I pride myself on making the things we sell.

Because each sales project is different, some summers are more prosperous than others. A lemon symbolizes our least successful project, the lemonade stand. Mom said "a lemonade stand is a timeless example of a first business." So, we decided to give it a try. But three of my neighbors had the same idea that year. It's hard to sell lemonade with that much competition!

Now we try more adventurous ideas. For example, this summer we sold homemade granola bars in unusual flavors. I got the idea from my favorite TV show, "International Snacks." On it, chefs speak in different dialects about how to make wholesome snacks from their homelands.

I was excited to try some of their recipes! And Abi thought granola bars would be easy to sell. He also managed to think of the perfect place to peddle them: his sister's ballgames. There we could sell without discrimination, targeting kids and parents alike!

Our granola bars were a huge hit! Everyone lavished praise on the unique flavors. Perhaps granola bars will have to be next year's sales project, too!

Concept Vocabulary

Think about the word *renaissance*. How could you start a renaissance? What kind of renaissance would it be?

Extend Vocabulary

In your Writer's Notebook, write a paragraph that describes one of the following:

- an *international* tour
- a *prosperous* family
- an object whose appeal is *timeless*

Read this Social Studies Connection. You will answer the questions as a class.

Text Feature

A **map** shows the relationship between different places.

Migrations

In "The Harlem Renaissance," you learned about the Great Migration North. Migrations like that have happened for many reasons. In the 1800s, thousands of people migrated west. Some were in search of gold and flocked to California. Some were in search of land and settled in places like Oklahoma and North Dakota. Some were escaping religious persecution, and some were seeking adventure. No matter their reason, they saw the wide open spaces of the west as a chance for a better life.

Some migrations are even international. In the 1970s, many people from Southeast Asia came to the United States as war refugees. Many settled in California and Texas. The first people to come sent word to others, and before long there was a community where people felt comfortable.

In the 1990s, people interested in working with computers moved to places such as Silicon Valley in California or Seattle, Washington. Several computer companies had started in those places and attracted people from all over.

Whatever the reason, migrations will continue today and for years to come.

During the Great Migration, thousands of African Americans left the south and settled in northern cities like New York, Chicago, Detroit, and St. Louis.

1. How does the map help you understand the Great Migration North?

2. Why do you live where you live? Did your parents, grandparents, or great grandparents move there for a reason?

3. Why do you think people like to live with other people from their culture? What are the advantages and the disadvantages of this?

 Go Digital

Search for the name of your town and the word "demographics" to learn about the people who live in your town. To what group do you belong?

Genre Historical Fiction

Essential Questions
Why would somebody move to a new community? Who were the first people to live in your community? What obstacles did they overcome?

The Overlanders

by Jason D. Nemeth
illustrated by Thaw Naing

Council Bluffs,

Iowa

April 3, 1853

Dear Tabitha,

It's been two days since we said good-bye. We are now in Council Bluffs waiting to get on the ferry. There are many, many wagons ahead of us. Ever since gold was discovered, it's as if the whole world is headed west.

I wish you were here with us. Since you're not, I've decided to keep a diary for you. I'll mail it when we arrive in Oregon City. I hope that reading it will help you know what lies ahead when you come next spring.

Your friend,
Ellie

⋆⇌ **April 6** ⇌⋆

Our turn to cross the Missouri River came today. We went on a steamer with 11 other wagons. I'm glad we didn't take one of the small ferries. I saw one lose some of its cargo, and I felt sad for the family who'd lost some of their things before their journey had even started.

⟶ April 21 ⟵

We've been on the trail for two weeks. Every day is the same.

We wake before sunrise. I help Ma with breakfast. Pa and Uncle William get the oxen and put a yoke around their necks. After breakfast (bread and bacon) we get going. Ma and I walk, but Billy rides in the wagon. He is too little to walk.

We stop at five o'clock and form the wagons into a circle to corral the animals. Then we set up our tent and make supper—more bread and bacon! After supper, everyone sits around the fire telling stories until bedtime. That's the best part of the day. By going through this together, we have all become very close.

⊷══ **April 25** ══⊷

We were delayed at Fort Kearney. Uncle William got sick just before our arrival. Several others in our wagon train were also sick. But Uncle William is now well, and we have set off again.

⊷══ **May 10** ══⊷

This journey is hard. We walk all day, no matter what the weather. We have hardly any fresh food. On the other hand, as Pa says when I grumble, we are lucky to be starting a new life in a new land.

⊷══ **May 17** ══⊷

The weather is hot, and I am often parched—but the sights help me forget how thirsty I am! Today I saw the strangest rock. It rose high above the prairie, like a tall chimney. You'll know it when you see it!

⊶═◯ May 20 ◯═⊷

Until now we haven't seen any other people. However, today a group of Pawnee rode up to our wagon train. At first we were concerned about what they might want. They just wanted to trade.

Pa traded some bacon for a pair of moccasins for me because my shoes are worn out.

⊶═◯ May 26 ◯═⊷

Fort Laramie at last! We will rest here for three days. It's hard to believe that only one-third of our journey is behind us. I am already tired of the trail.

One of the families in our wagon train is staying here. The Johnsons have decided their children are too young to trek all the way to the West.

⤙⤏ May 31 ⤎⤗

The trail is littered with all kinds of things. Today we passed an oak desk, a dresser, a set of china, and a stove. The oxen are tired and thirsty. They cannot pull such heavy loads, so people have to abandon their treasures along the way.

⤙⤏ June 20 ⤎⤗

Today we passed Independence Rock. I carved my name into the rock. We looked at the names of those who have already passed along the trail. Even though we had never met, I felt connected to them.

⤙⤏ June 30 ⤎⤗

We went through South Pass yesterday. We are so tired, yet half the journey still lies ahead. Ma says many people are worse off than we are. Some could not afford oxen, so they pull their carts themselves.

Low Bridge

by Thomas S. Allen
illustrated by Brian Deines

I've got an old mule and her name is Sal,
Fifteen miles on the Erie Canal.
She's a good old worker and a good old pal,
Fifteen miles on the Erie Canal.
We've hauled some barges in our day
Filled with lumber, coal, and hay,
And every inch of the way we know
From Albany to Buffalo.

Low bridge, everybody down.
Low bridge for we're coming to a town.
And you'll always know your neighbor,
And you'll always know your pal,
If you've ever navigated on the Erie Canal.

We'd better get along on our way, old gal,
Fifteen miles on the Erie Canal.
'Cause you bet your life I'd never part with Sal,
Fifteen miles on the Erie Canal.
Git up there mule, here comes a lock,
We'll make Rome 'bout six o'clock,
One more trip and back we'll go,
Right back home to Buffalo.

Low bridge, everybody down.
Low bridge for we're coming to a town.
And you'll always know your neighbor,
And you'll always know your pal,
If you've ever navigated on the Erie Canal.

You will answer the comprehension questions on these pages as a class.

Text Connections

1. Why does Ellie's family leave their home and travel to Oregon?

2. What hardships does Ellie experience or see on the trip? Find evidence in the text that supports your answer.

3. How did the people who traveled the Oregon Trail help change America?

4. What does Ellie's family have in common with Mei and Hong in "A New Life for Mei" and the people who were part of the Great Migration North in "The Harlem Renaissance"?

Did You Know?

Oregon and Washington are as far north as Maine, but they do not have extreme cold weather with snow and ice in the winter. That's because weather moves from west to east and the Pacific Ocean keeps the climate warmer in the winter and cooler in the summer.

Look Closer

Keys to Comprehension

1. Why do people have to leave things along the trail?

2. Do Ellie's parents have positive attitudes? Use evidence from the text to explain why or why not.

Writer's Craft

3. What do you think the term *cargo* means? What evidence in the text supports your conclusion?

4. Why do you think Ellie "felt connected" to the others who carved their names into Independence Rock? Do you think you would feel the same way? Explain your answer.

Concept Development

5. How does the illustration on pages 366–367 clarify what is happening in the song "Low Bridge"?

Write

Write a message to a friend about a trip you took. Where did you go? How long did it take? What did you do on your trip?

Read the story.
Then discuss it
with your class.

Vocabulary Words

- **abandon**
- **acres**
- **ferry**
- **territory**
- **trade**
- **yoke**

Changes Coming

Jackson stared out his bedroom window at the abandoned field behind his house. Until a couple years ago, it was planted with corn or beans, depending on the summer. But now it was overgrown with long grass, spindly maple saplings, and wildflowers. According to a rumor, the field's owner had sold these acres. Soon a developer would make the land useful again by building on it.

The open territory around Jackson's home would someday be very different. Jackson hoped it would become a new neighborhood of homes. Then there might be new friends living near enough that he could ride his bike to see them.

But Jackson had mixed feelings about the coming changes. According to a proud family legend, his great-grandfather had been one of the first farmers here many years ago. His great-grandfather came up from the South and ferried all his belongings across the Ohio River.

Then he continued north. Finally he found a plot of rich, dark soil. He traded some family silver for a plow and then set to working the earth. With the help of just one yoke of oxen, he broke the ground and planted the first of many corn crops.

Jackson wondered how the field had looked before it was farmed. He imagined it much like the way it looked today, a tangle of leaves and brush. Now it would be tamed again, this time with bricks and concrete. It would be interesting to see what the changes would bring!

Concept Vocabulary

Think about the word *pioneer*. How did pioneers settle the area around you? Are there still pioneers today?

Extend Vocabulary

Copy the word web into your Writer's Notebook. Then fill it in with the names of different types of things that people can *trade*.

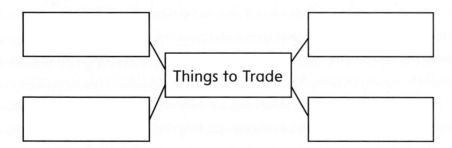

Read this Social Studies Connection. You will answer the questions as a class.

Text Feature

A **chart** helps people compare information in an organized way.

How Am I Like You?

When you read "The Overlanders," you met Ellie. She is writing a diary that she is going to send to her best friend, Tabitha. In her diary, Ellie describes what she sees. She describes how her body feels when she is tired or thirsty. She also tells about her emotions, including when she is grumpy, sad, or happy.

Ellie's story is set over 150 years ago. She experiences things that nobody her age would likely experience now. But even if you do not have the same experiences as someone else, you can still share similar feelings or interests.

Think about how you and Ellie are similar. What interests do you and Ellie have in common? Would you behave the same or differently if you took four months to travel across the country?

Now think about how you and the real people in your life are similar. How are you and your friends or siblings alike? How are you different? What are you good at doing? What are others good at doing? Make a chart of your likes, dislikes, and abilities. Compare your chart with two other students in your class. How are you similar to them? How are you unique?

	likes	dislikes	abilities
me			
classmate 1			
classmate 2			

1. Look at the chart you made. What interests do you share with your classmates? What interests do you have that are less common?

2. What kinds of experiences do all people share?

3. What experiences or abilities make you a unique person?

 Go Digital

Search for information about what your community was like in the past. How is it similar to today? How is it different? How are the people from the past the same as you? How are they different?

Genre Informational Text

Essential Questions

What impact have Native Americans had on this country? How were early Native American communities forced to change?

The Cherokee: Gold and Tears

by Jessica Lasko

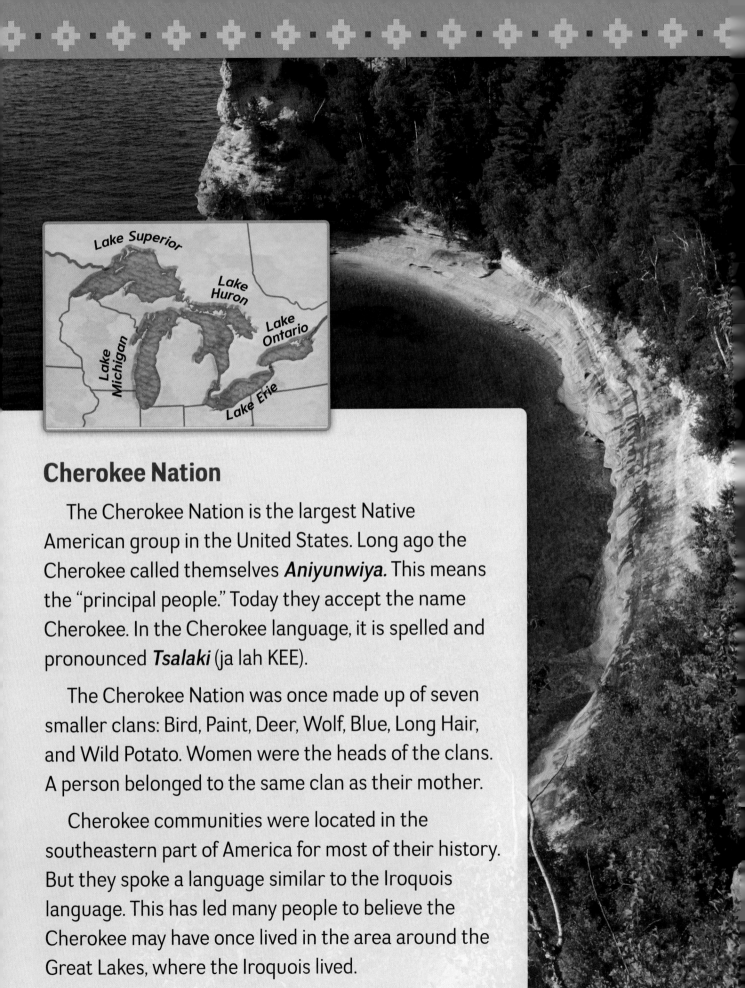

Cherokee Nation

The Cherokee Nation is the largest Native American group in the United States. Long ago the Cherokee called themselves *Aniyunwiya.* This means the "principal people." Today they accept the name Cherokee. In the Cherokee language, it is spelled and pronounced *Tsalaki* (ja lah KEE).

The Cherokee Nation was once made up of seven smaller clans: Bird, Paint, Deer, Wolf, Blue, Long Hair, and Wild Potato. Women were the heads of the clans. A person belonged to the same clan as their mother.

Cherokee communities were located in the southeastern part of America for most of their history. But they spoke a language similar to the Iroquois language. This has led many people to believe the Cherokee may have once lived in the area around the Great Lakes, where the Iroquois lived.

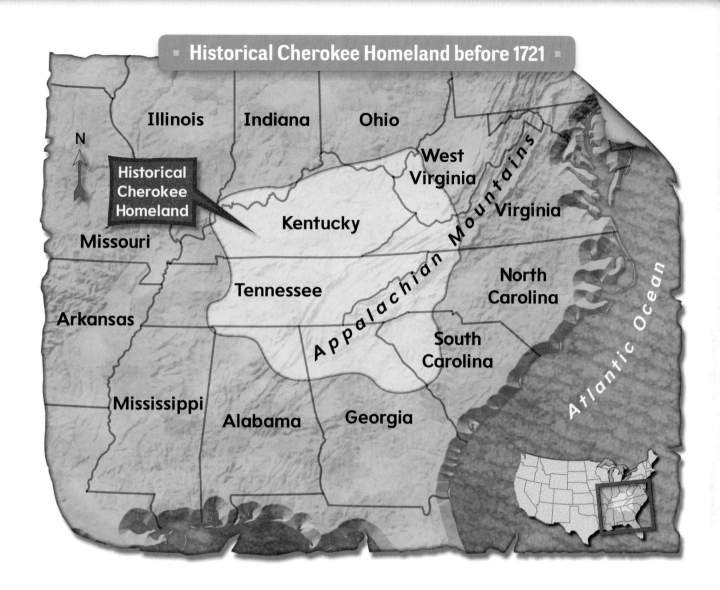

Historical Cherokee Homeland before 1721

Illinois Indiana Ohio

N

Historical Cherokee Homeland

West Virginia

Virginia

Kentucky

Appalachian Mountains

Missouri

North Carolina

Tennessee

Arkansas

South Carolina

Atlantic Ocean

Mississippi

Alabama Georgia

Wars with the Iroquois and the Delaware groups may have caused the Cherokee to migrate southeast many hundreds of years ago.

The Cherokee made their new home in the Appalachian Mountains. They lived in most of present-day Kentucky and Tennessee. They were also present in parts of Virginia, West Virginia, Ohio, Indiana, Georgia, Alabama, North Carolina, and South Carolina.

Meeting the Europeans

The first contact the Cherokee had with Europeans was in 1540. The Spanish explorer Hernando de Soto passed briefly through some of their villages. He and his men were in search of gold.

In 1654, the first English explorers arrived in the southern Appalachian Mountains.

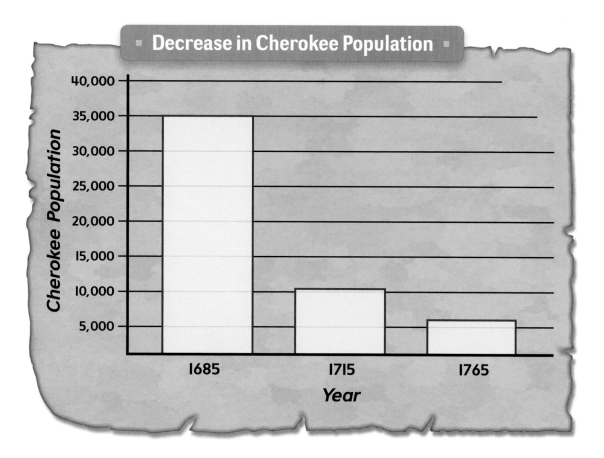

Decrease in Cherokee Population

Cherokee Population

40,000
35,000
30,000
25,000
20,000
15,000
10,000
5,000

1685   1715   1765

Year

At the time, there were many southeastern Native American tribes. However, the Cherokee Nation was one of the largest and most powerful. In the early 1600s, about 22,500 people lived on Cherokee lands.

Soon English colonists came to Cherokee lands to trade. They gave guns and metal tools to the Cherokee. In return the Cherokee traded animal skins. By the 1670s, the traders were coming all the time.

During the 1700s, many Cherokee people fell sick due to smallpox. The disease came to America with the settlers. The Cherokee had never seen the disease before. At first only a few Cherokee became sick, but the smallpox soon spread through their communities. The sickness killed one-third to one-half of all Cherokee people.

Changing Ways

By the 1800s, the Cherokee began to take on American and European culture. They began to dress like the new settlers. Soon they were building homes and farms that resembled those of the settlers.

In 1820, the Cherokee formed a type of government. The government was modeled after the United States government. The Cherokee had a principal chief. They also had a senate and a house of representatives.

The next year, the Cherokee developed a way of writing, too. A silversmith named Sequoyah (sih KWOY uh) designed characters for the Cherokee alphabet. He felt it was important for the tribe to read and write in Cherokee.

The Cherokee quickly became a literate people. Being able to read and write helped them prosper in many ways.

A Cherokee constitution was written in 1827. The next year, the first Native American newspaper was started. It was named the **Cherokee Phoenix** and was written in both English and Cherokee.

Later that year, gold was discovered in Cherokee land. But this was not a fortunate discovery for the Cherokee. Within ten years, their homeland would no longer be theirs.

Trail of Tears Migration, 1838-1839

UNITED STATES

Ohio River

Springfield · Missouri · Kentucky

Tahlequah

Nashville

Tennessee River

Evansville

Appalachian Mountains

Fort Gibson

Indian Territory

Memphis

Arkansas River

Tennessee

Mississippi River

Charleston
Fort Payne

Arkansas

MEXICO

Mississippi

Alabama

Cherokee Tribal Territory

Georgia

Trail of Tears

When gold was found in northern Georgia in 1828, there was a great surge in the number of settlers. Many settlers wanted to mine for gold on Cherokee land. Georgia's state government passed a law to take the land away from the Cherokee. The Cherokee challenged that law. The case went all the way to the U.S. Supreme Court.

The Supreme Court ruled in favor of the Cherokee and said they could not be removed from their land unless they agreed to it.

In the end though, it did not keep the Cherokee from being forced from their land.

In 1835 a small group of Cherokee agreed to sign a treaty. They gave up their land for $5,700.00. The agreement also gave the Cherokee tribe land in Indian Territory, in present-day Oklahoma.

rth
olina

ATLANTIC
OCEAN

N

Trail of Tears water route
Trail of Tears land route

Most of the Cherokee people did not agree with this. But U.S. troops went into Cherokee country anyway. In the winter of 1838-1839, the Cherokee were forced from their homes by the U.S. Army.

The Cherokee made the long journey west to Indian Territory in winter. They had little food. Nearly one-fourth of the Cherokee people died during this forced migration. This terrible journey came to be known as the Trail of Tears.

A story says that one night the chiefs prayed for a sign to lift the spirits of the crying mothers. The chiefs knew there was no hope for the Cherokee if the women were too sad and weak to care for their children.

The next morning, the chiefs told the mothers to look back on the trail. Where tears had dropped, roses now bloomed.

The roses had seven leaves on each stem, like the seven clans of the Cherokee. The center of each rose was golden, like the gold taken from the Cherokee community. Today the Cherokee rose is the state flower of Georgia.

Essential Questions
What is the history of your community?
Does that history affect you now?

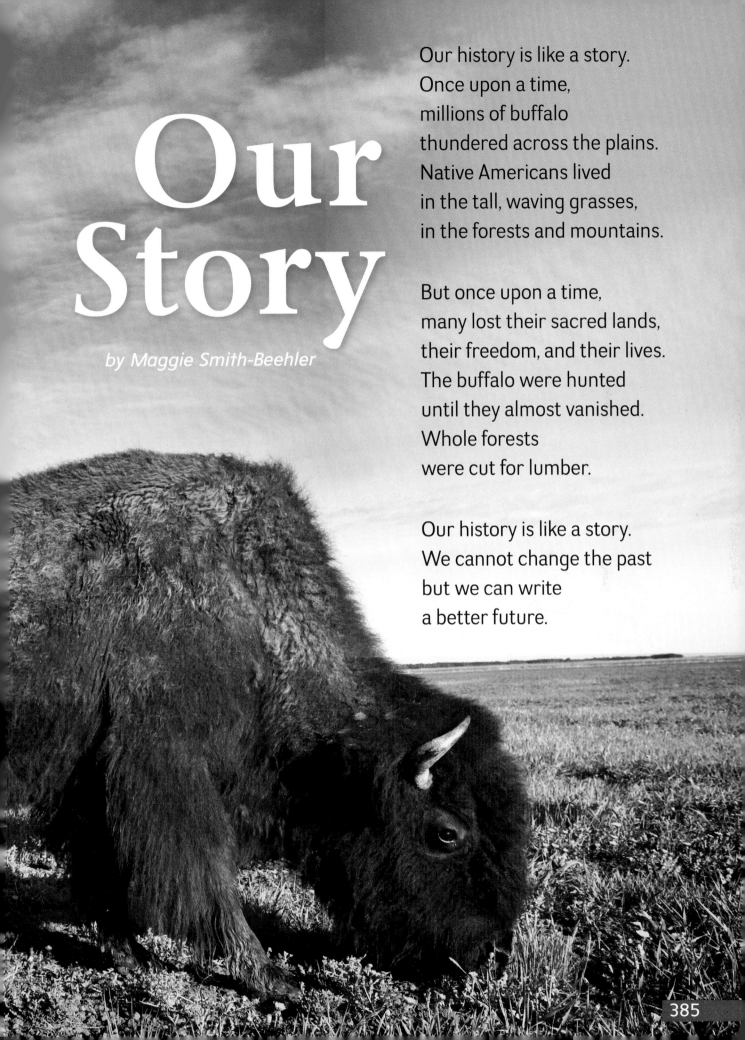

Our Story

by Maggie Smith-Beehler

Our history is like a story.
Once upon a time,
millions of buffalo
thundered across the plains.
Native Americans lived
in the tall, waving grasses,
in the forests and mountains.

But once upon a time,
many lost their sacred lands,
their freedom, and their lives.
The buffalo were hunted
until they almost vanished.
Whole forests
were cut for lumber.

Our history is like a story.
We cannot change the past
but we can write
a better future.

You will answer the comprehension questions on these pages as a class.

Text Connections

1. In what ways did Europeans affect the Cherokee culture?

2. What was the Trail of Tears? Do you think *Trail of Tears* is a good name for the journey? Why or why not?

3. How did the movement of the Cherokee change the nation?

4. Contrast how the Cherokee moved to Oklahoma with how the people in the other stories in this unit moved.

Did You Know?

Between June and December 1838, more than 15,000 Cherokee walked over a thousand miles to Oklahoma.

Look Closer

Keys to Comprehension

1. How did the Cherokee try to get along with the other people in the United States?

2. What sequence of events led to the U.S. Army forcing the Cherokee to move?

Writer's Craft

3. What does the subtitle "Gold and Tears" mean?

4. How many different routes were used by the Cherokee to reach Indian Territory? How do you know?

Concept Development

5. Compare the Oregon Trail of "The Overlanders" to the Trail of Tears.

Write

Trace the Trail of Tears on a map. Write about some of the hardships the Cherokee might have faced on each route.

Read this Social Studies Connection. You will answer the questions as a class.

Text Feature

A **caption** tells about a picture and adds information to an article or story.

Changing Culture

Today, the Cherokee culture in Oklahoma combines the customs of their ancestors with a modern lifestyle. The *Cherokee Phoenix* is still published, in both English and Cherokee characters. The Cherokee Heritage Center features numerous exhibits and shows. These reflect the traditions and history of Cherokee culture.

As today's Cherokee Nation shows, cultures grow and change over time. Changes occur as new technologies affect the way people communicate, work, and live. Changing environments can change what people eat and where they live. When people travel or move to a new place, they see different customs. They also take their own customs with them and can introduce different ways of doing things.

A culture is flexible and can adapt. Culture is reflected in clothing, music, food, and buildings. But more importantly, it is reflected in beliefs and values. Even as a culture like the Cherokee changes, there will always be a link to the past through the beliefs and values each generation shares.

A member of the Cherokee Nation in the 1800s.

A member of the Cherokee Nation today.

1. How can cultures change over time?

2. Compare the two images above. What are some of the differences in culture between the two? What do you think they share?

3. How do the captions for these images add to your understanding? What if they were not included?

 Go Digital

Search for information about the history of clothing. Find pictures of what types of clothes people wore at different times. Then search for "cultural foods." What foods do people of different cultures eat that you have never tried?

Genre Biography

Essential Questions

Why do people want to feel like part of a community? How can a community work together to overcome hardship?

The Dancing Bird of Paradise

by Renée S. Sanford
illustrated by Cheryl Kirk Noll

Seven-year-old Haruno's black eyes sparkled with delight. Her cousin Yuki's kimono swished and flared to the lilting Japanese music. The year was 1931, and fifteen-year-old Yuki was visiting her grandfather's farm in a beautiful valley near San Francisco, California.

That evening, the community was performing a kabuki play. A kabuki play is a style of Japanese theater that tells stories with song and dance. The old hall would be filled with Japanese farmers and their families. They now lived in America but still enjoyed the costumes and drama of kabuki.

Yuki had learned several native Japanese dances and planned to perform at intermission.

"Come, Haruno," Yuki beckoned to her small cousin. "You may be young, but you are big enough to learn this dance." Haruno jumped up and followed Yuki's every move with her head and hands, just as she had followed her with her eyes.

A gentleman from the big city was watching and was impressed. "This child has tremendous talent," he told Haruno's mother. "She should go to the Tachibana Dance School in Tokyo. She will learn the beautiful Japanese dances and become a great dancer."

Haruno knew only that she loved to dance, but her parents did not forget the gentleman's words. Five years later, she boarded a ship with her grandparents and returned to Japan. Each day she went to school and then to her dance lesson. She stayed longer each time, watching the other students, learning their dances as well as her own.

Sometimes Haruno was lonely for her family. She wrote them letters about her life in Japan. Then her cousins would come to visit, and the days would be filled with fun and laughter. It was just like being back home.

One day, Grandfather called for Haruno to come and speak with him.

"Haruno," he said, "it is time for you to go home. Things are changing. Very soon I feel that Japan and the United States may be at war."

Haruno was startled. She loved both of her countries; how could they ever fight each other? But she knew Grandfather was wise and that she must listen to him.

Grandfather continued, "Before you go, you must receive your dancing name. You have worked long and hard for it. I want you to take back to America something valuable from your time in Japan."

The very next week, Haruno stood poised before the headmaster of the dance school. As soon as he nodded, she began to dance with all her heart and skill. Her dance teacher came to her side. "My name is Saho—bird of paradise—and I have taught you well. So I give you a name that shows you are my student. You will be Sahomi Tachibana—a beautiful bird of paradise who learned to dance at Tachibana."

In November 1941, Haruno—Sahomi—sailed back to her home in California. Within a few weeks the United States and Japan were fighting in World War II.

Overnight the Japanese people living in America were accused of being spies. Japanese Americans looked different from most other Americans. Many people in the United States had never met a Japanese person. Because of this, non-Asian Americans were afraid Japanese Americans might help Japan in the war. Japanese Americans loved their new country and were very loyal. Even so, the United States government ordered them to move from the West Coast. They were to be sent to internment camps.

DAILY NEWS

NEW YORK'S PICTURE NEWSPAPER

FINAL

Copr. 1941 by News Syndicate Co. Inc.

Trade Mark Reg. U. S. Pat. Off.

Average net paid circulation for November exceeded
Daily --- 1,925,000
Sunday - 3,750,000

Vol. 23. No. 142

New York, Monday, December 8, 1941★

64 Main + 4 Manhattan Pages

2 Cents IN CITY LIMITS | 3 CENTS Elsewhere

JAPAN AT WAR WITH U.S.

∧ Tanforan Assembly Center

It was not fair, but Sahomi knew they had no
other choice. Her family had lived as good, orderly
citizens. In a good and orderly way, they boarded
the bus that took them to the distant Tanforan
Assembly Center.

When they arrived, Sahomi choked back a
feeling of sickness as she looked around. The
center had been a racetrack, and the smell of
horses still hung heavily in the air. The old stalls
had been converted into places for people to live.

After a few months, Sahomi and the other Japanese Americans were put on a train to Utah. Three days later they arrived at the Topaz Relocation Center. Like Tanforan, this internment camp was far different from Sahomi's comfortable home. Families crowded into long rows of barrack apartments. Each room was lit by a single bulb hanging in the middle of the ceiling. They were heated by potbellied stoves that burned coal and wood. Only the latrines and laundry rooms had running water. Families shared meals at long tables in a large dining hall. They had to report for roll call each morning.

⌄ Topaz Relocation Center

Eventually, over 8,000 people came to live in the Topaz Relocation Center. The unfairly imprisoned Japanese Americans attempted to live a normal life. They tried to improve their new community. They planted gardens, created schools, and opened a hospital. Many brave young men joined the Army to fight for the country which had treated them so poorly. Despite their efforts, life was not easy for Sahomi and the other internees.

Because they were living in the middle of the Sevier Desert, they sweltered through the blistering summer heat. During dust storms, fine sand blew through the cracks in the walls. It coated the few belongings that Sahomi and her family had brought with them.

The people still enjoyed being entertained, so they asked whoever had a talent to share it. "Please teach our children to dance," some parents asked Sahomi. Once again, Sahomi had a stage on which to perform. *This was not what I expected,* she thought, *but I can still share the dances of Japan with people around me. If I ever want to be a professional, I can never stop dancing. Even when life is hard and unfair.*

The children at Topaz went to school in the internment camp. After class, an eager group would gather around Sahomi. She patiently taught them the delicate steps of the dances that were as familiar as her own thoughts. When she taught her students, Sahomi explained the story behind each dance.

After much practice, her students were ready for their first recital. Because of the oppressive summer heat, the children did not dress in traditional heavy kimonos. "You may be dressed simply," Sahomi told them, "but you must dance your very best. Make the beauty of the land and stories of Japan come alive to everyone who sees you." Parents and friends smiled their appreciation as they were transported to a different, more beautiful time through the children's dances. For a brief period, Sahomi and the other dancers brought the community together. Life felt normal for a change.

^ Carnegie Hall

After three long years, the American government realized what a terrible mistake it had made. The war was ending, and the Japanese American people were allowed to live where they wished. Sahomi's father wanted to see what the East Coast was like, so the family moved to Pennsylvania. At first, she could only get a job as a cook, even though she didn't really know how to cook. But she kept taking dance lessons and kept performing and teaching.

Then Sahomi took a big step—she moved to New York City and began classes at Studio 61 in Carnegie Hall. Like the brilliant bird of paradise, she donned beautiful costumes and shone brighter than any dancer of her kind.

Sahomi began teaching privately, but her talent was no secret. One day, Eleanor Roosevelt, the president's wife, came to see her perform. Then, in 1966, Sahomi started her own Tachibana Dance School in New York City.

Several times Sahomi traveled to Japan to learn more dances. Like she had in Topaz, she shared these dances with her community when she returned. Everywhere Sahomi went, people loved to watch her graceful performances. They did not look down on her anymore because she was Japanese. They knew that she had a gift to share with them.

What a beautiful gift it is!

You will answer the comprehension questions on these pages as a class.

Text Connections

1. Why is Haruno given the name "Sahomi"?

2. After leaving Topaz, what is the "big step" that Sahomi takes? Why is it a big step?

3. What impact do the photographs of Tanforan and Topaz have on your understanding of this selection?

4. Why did the people of Topaz build things like schools and hospitals?

Did You Know?

Over 100,000 people of Japanese ancestry were relocated by the U.S. government during World War II. In 1988, the government formally apologized to the internees and their descendants.

Look Closer

Keys to Comprehension

1. Why were Sahomi and other Japanese Americans interned at Topaz?

2. Why do the people of Topaz ask Sahomi to teach their children to dance?

Writer's Craft

3. What does the word *overnight* on page 398 mean? Why do you think the author uses that word?

Concept Development

4. How does the description of the recital Sahomi and the children put on connect to the description of life at Topaz?

5. Compare what happened to Sahomi and the other Japanese-American internees with what happened to the Cherokee. How were the events similar? How were they different?

Write

Imagine you are living back in 1942. Write an opinion newspaper article explaining why it is unfair to imprison loyal Japanese Americans at places like Tanforan and Topaz.

Genre Historical Fiction

Essential Questions
What is the oldest thing in your neighborhood?
What in your community reminds you of the
past? What effect can you have on your
community's future?

Arbor Day Square

by Kathryn O. Galbraith
illustrated by Cyd Moore

"Hmmm." Katie takes a deep breath.

"Everything smells new," she tells Papa.

And everything does.

Their prairie town is growing week by week. Now they have stores with glass windows. A church with a steeple. And a schoolhouse with desks for all seventeen students to sit in long rows.

Every week the train brings more people who are eager for land.

The train also brings more lumber and logs for houses, stables, fences, and barns.

Papa helps pace out the town square. It will be a gathering place for concerts. And socials. And speeches. Like the squares back East, the ones back home, the ones they remember as children.

Only one thing is missing. Katie and the children know it. The townsfolk and farmers know it too.

There are no trees on the prairie.

No trees for climbing.

Or for shade.

No trees for fruit or warm winter fires.

No trees for birds. Or for beauty.

419

At the town meeting, everyone agrees that a proper town—their town—*needs* trees.

Mrs. Johanson passes a basket. Precious nickels, dimes, and quarters tumble in. *Jingle, jingle, clink.* Katie adds her own six pennies and Papa's silver dollar.

When the basket is heavy, Mr. Klein taps out an order over the telegraph lines.

SEND 15 TREES

Days tick by. Sunny days. Rainy days. Windy days when dust devils dance in the road. At last the telegraph lines tap back:

TREES ARE COMING

TOOO-OOOOOOOOOOOO!

When the train pulls in, folks hurry to the depot. Babies and dogs come too. Katie skips beside Papa, swinging her bucket and Dolly.

They're here!

Papa, Mr. Zimmerman, and all the O'Briens carefully unload the boxcar, counting as they go. "...thirteen, fourteen, fifteen!"

Katie stares at the saplings, spindly and green. "They're too little!"

"Don't worry. They'll grow," promises Papa.

But Katie isn't sure.

Katie and Papa follow the parade of trees to the new town square.

Papa and Mister Carter dig three holes.

Dig, swing, scoop.

Dig, swing, scoop.

Papa plants three small maples.

"Let me help," Katie says. She gently pats the soil down around each baby tree.

Under the warm sun, more trees spring up.

"Someday, these oaks will shade the bench," Papa says. "And there, the elm tree will shelter the bandstand."

But Katie isn't sure.

Neighbors plant four maples near the church.

One apple tree on the corner.

And three chestnut trees in the dusty school yard.

Danny O'Brien leads the bucket brigade.

Katie lugs her bucket too.

Cool drinks for thirsty trees.

And dogs.

In a quiet corner of the Square, Papa and Katie dig a hole together. Here they plant a flowering dogwood, in memory of Mama.

Katie touches the tender leaves. It is very little, but…

"Now this is *our* special tree," she whispers.

Papa hugs her. "Yes, our *very* special tree."

As the sun begins to set, the Square bristles and blooms with greens. Papa and Katie spread their blanket next to Mama's tree.

Katie peeks into the basket.

There's plenty of food

to share with friends

and dogs.

And Dolly.

As old Doc fiddles up the moon, neighbors gather their children and dogs and wave goodnight.

"Let's do this again next year."

And they do. Year after year they gather in the Square for another Arbor Day, a tree planting day, a holiday.

Carrying shovels, rakes, and hoes, Katie and Papa help plant trees throughout the town.

Trees for climbing.

And for shade.

Trees for fruit and warm winter fires.

Trees for birds.

And for beauty.

And every year Papa laughs and tells Katie,

"Don't worry, honey. They'll grow."

And every year they do.

It's another Arbor Day. Neighbors, kids, and dogs hurry to the Square.

Here come Katie and Danny O'Brien with their Megan Anne. Katie's papa—now a grandpa—holds one of Megan's hands.

In the Square lies a small row of saplings, spindly and green.

Katie smiles. "One day that willow will sweep the pond," she says. "And there, the cedar will sweep the sky."

Megan shakes her head and Katie laughs. "Don't worry, honey. They'll grow. Now, let's find your Grandma's tree."

Megan runs across the Square. Her family follows just behind.

There Katie spreads out their blanket under the blooming dogwood tree. Robins rustle in the leaves. Sparrows chirp and flutter.

Megan peeks into the basket. There's plenty of food to share with friends, and dogs. And Bear.

When the moon rises, silver and round, neighbors gather up children and grandchildren and whistle for the dogs. "See you here again next year," they call.

And they do.

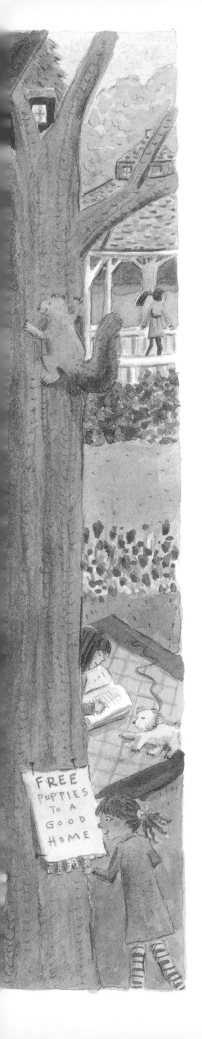

Celebrating
families,
trees,
and
neighbors.
Year after year.
And the year after that.

You will answer the comprehension questions on these pages as a class.

Text Connections

1. Why do the townspeople want to plant trees in their growing town?

2. What types of trees do the settlers first plant?

3. How does their Arbor Day tradition help bring the community together? Use evidence from the text to explain your answer.

4. How does "The Overlanders" compare to this story?

Did You Know?

Dutch Elm disease, caused by a fungus and spread by a type of beetle, was found in New England in 1928 and began moving through the rest of North America. By 1989, over three quarters of the elm trees had died.

Look Closer

Keys to Comprehension

1. Why does it take so long for the trees to arrive?

2. What kind of person is Papa? How can you tell?

Writer's Craft

3. *Arbor* is a Latin word that means "tree." What clues on page 435 help you understand what the word *arbor* means?

4. How would you feel about planting trees if you were Katie?

Concept Development

5. How do the illustrations help you understand the time frame of the story? How does the time pass in this story?

Write

Write a description of a tree you would want to plant on Arbor Day. What type of tree would it be? What would it look like?

**Read the story.
Then discuss it
with your class.**

Vocabulary Words

- **blooming**
- **brigade**
- **bristles**
- **deep**
- **depot**
- **order**
- **precious**
- **rustle**
- **saplings**
- **spindly**
- **stables**
- **sweep**

A Fine Welcome Home

Camp had been fun, but now Charlie was deeply anxious to get home. All he could think about was his horse, Daisy, who was due to give birth at any time. Charlie paced in front of the bus depot until his older brother, Steven, came to pick him up.

"Has the baby come yet?" Charlie asked, as he hopped in the car.

"Not yet," Steven replied. Charlie drummed his fingers on the car door as Steven pulled out from the depot.

It was a warm day, so the boys rolled down their windows to enjoy the fresh air. As they neared their family's farm, Charlie caught the scent of honeysuckle blooming in the pasture.

"I know you want to visit Daisy, but we'd better say hi to the kitchen brigade first," Steven said to Charlie. Charlie's other siblings were helping their mom fix supper. Charlie went to the house to greet them and hug his mom hello.

"Would you like to order a special dinner, Charlie?" his mother asked.

"No, thanks," Charlie replied. "How is Daisy doing?"

His mom smiled. "Go see for yourself, Charlie."

Charlie ran out to Daisy's stable and arrived to find a new little colt rustling to its feet. The colt's legs were spindly, like the trunks of small saplings. Daisy nudged the colt with her nose, to help him find his balance. Then she swept the fine bristles on the back of his neck with her tongue.

Charlie grinned widely at the precious sight. "You did great, Daisy!" he said joyously. "Just like I knew you would."

Concept Vocabulary

Think about the word *tradition*. What are some of your favorite traditions? Who taught you about them?

Extend Vocabulary

Answer and explain the following questions with a partner.

- Do you think a family photo album would be a **precious** possession?
- In which season are most plants **blooming?**
- Where are some places you might find **stables?**

Read this Science Connection. You will answer the questions as a class.

Text Feature

Italic text is used to emphasize an important word.

Planting Trees

In "Arbor Day Square" the townsfolk and farmers know that something is missing—trees. For the settlers, this is very different from their homes in the eastern part of the country.

There are many reasons for the lack of trees. Long dry periods without rain is one reason. Fire is another possible cause. Without people to water them or put out fires, the trees would not survive.

When people plant trees, however, the environment changes. Not only can trees provide shade, fruit, and firewood for people, they provide habitats for animals.

Whenever we make changes to an environment, we must think about both the benefits *and* the potential problems. One potential problem that comes from planting trees on the prairie has to do with the bison. These enormous animals roam the prairie, eating the grasses that cover it. How might planting trees affect the bison? How can changes to the bison's habitat affect other plants and animals? These are the types of questions we must ask before making any environmental changes.

1. What word in the text is set in italics? Why do you think the author wanted to emphasize it?

2. How would changing the prairie into a forest affect the bison?

3. Imagine you are working with the settlers in "Arbor Day Square." They want to cover the prairie in trees. They also want to keep the bison happy. What solution would you suggest for this problem? What other options could you suggest?

 Go Digital

Search for pictures of "animals and plants that live in the prairie" and "animals and plants that live in trees." Compare the two different habitats. How does an environment change when trees are planted?

Glossary

abandon (ə ban´ dən) *v.* to give up something completely

accommodate (ə kom´ ə dāt´) *v.* to do a favor or service for; to help

accompany (ə kum´ pə nē) *v.* to happen in connection or combination with

accurate (ak´ yûr it) *adj.* without errors or mistakes

acres (ā´ kûrz) *n.* plural form of **acre:** a measure of land equal to 43,500 square feet

adventure (ad ven´ chûr) *n.* a thrilling or unusual experience; an exciting activity

alighted (ə līt´ id) *v.* a form of the verb **alight:** to land from flight

alley (al´ē) *n.* a narrow street or passageway, especially one at the rear of a row of buildings

alley

amazement (ə māz´ mənt) *n.* extreme wonder or surprise

ancestors (an´ ses tûrz) *n.* plural form of **ancestor:** someone from long ago in a direct relation to you

anchor (ang´ kûr) *v.* to fasten in place

Antarctic (ant ark´ tik) *adj.* relating to the South Pole or south polar regions

anxious (ang´ shəs) *adj.* uneasy, worried, or fearful about what may happen

appointed (ə poin´ tid) *v.* a form of the verb **appoint:** to decide on; set

apprehensive (ap´ rē hen´ siv) *adj.* fearful about what may happen; uneasy

assemble (ə sem´ bəl) *v.* to meet or come together

beckoned (bek´ ənd) *v.* a form of the verb **beckon:** to make a sign or signal by moving the hand or head

before (bi for´) *prep.* in front of *adv.* earlier than the time when

bellowed (bel´ ōd) *v.* a form of the verb **bellow:** to cry out in a loud, deep voice

blooming (blōō´ ming) *adj.* in flower; blossoming

brigade (bri gād´) *n.* a group of people organized for a specific purpose

bristles (bris´ əlz) *v.* a form of the verb **bristle:** to be full of or covered by something

cast (kast) *n.* the actors in a play or movie

ceremony (sâr´ ə mō´ nē) *n.* an act or acts done on a special or important occasion

characters (kar´ ik tûrz) *n.* plural form of **character:** a mark or sign used as a symbol in writing or printing

characters

快樂
Pleasure

circulating (sûr´ kyə lāt´ ing) *v.* a form of the verb **circulate:** to move around in the shape of a circle

classifications (klas´ ə fə kā´ shənz) *n.* plural form of **classification:** a specific, systematic arrangement of things into categories

cold (kōld) *adj.* not friendly or kind

common (kom´ ən) *adj.* often found

compete (kəm pēt´) *v.* to try to win a contest against others

concern (kən sûrn´) *n.* worried interest

confident (kon´ fi dənt) *adj.* having the belief that you can do something well or succeed

continent (kon´ tə nənt) *n.* one of the seven large land areas on the planet

converted (kən vûrt id) *v.* a form of the verb **convert:** to change from one thing to another thing

cottage (kot´ ij) *n.* a small house, usually in the country or in a summer resort

cottage

cover (kuv´ ûr) *n.* protection or shelter

crisp (krisp) *adj.* keen and bracing; brisk; invigorating

criticize (crit´ ə sīz´) *v.* to find fault with something

deep (dēp) *adj.* great in degree; intense

delicate (del´i kət) *adj.* finely skilled or sensitive

demolish (di mol´ish) *v.* to tear down or apart; to destroy the structure of

depot (dē´ pō) *n.* a railroad station or bus terminal

deserted (di zûrt´ id) *adj.* without humans

dialect (dī´ ə lekt) *n.* language that is spoken in a particular area or by a particular group and differs from other forms of the same language

discrimination (di skrim´ ə nā´ shən) *n.* unfair difference in treatment; prejudice

dissipates (di´ sə pāts´) *v.* a form of the verb **dissipate:** to disperse or scatter; to be dispelled

distant (dis´ tənt) *adj.* far off or away

donned (dond) *v.* a form of the verb **don:** to put on

douse (dous) *v.* to throw a liquid on; drench

drive (drīv) *v.* to frighten or prod an animal or animals into moving in a desired direction

droughts (drouts) *n.* plural form of **drought:** a long period of dry weather

dusk (dusk) *n.* the time of day just before nightfall

dusk

elaborate (i lab´ ûr it) *adj.* worked out or made with great care and detail

elegant (el´ i gənt) *adj.* showing refined beauty

elevation (el´ ə vā´ shən) *n.* the height above sea level

evaporate (i vap´ ə rāt) *v.* to change from a liquid or solid into a gas

evening (ēv´ ning) *n.* the time following afternoon and continuing through early nighttime

451

Pronunciation Key: at; lāte; câre; fäther; set; mē; it; kīte; ox; rōse; ô in bought; coin; book; too; form; out; up; ūse; tûrn; ə sound in about, chicken, pencil cannon, circus; chair; ring; shop; thin; there; zh in treasure.

examined (eg zam´ ind) *v.* a form of the verb **examine:** to look at closely and carefully; inspect

exhausted (eks ôs´ tid) *adj.* very weak or tired

exhausted

experience (ek´ spēr´ ē´ əns) *v.* to do or see something or have something happen to you

extinct (ek stingkt´) *adj.* no longer active or burning

fame (fām) *n.* a widespread reputation, especially for great achievement

fate (fāt) *n.* unavoidable lot or fortune; destiny

ferry (fâr´ ē) *n.* a boat used to carry people, cars, and goods across a narrow body of water

flared (flârd) *v.* a form of the verb **flare:** to open or spread outward

flow (flō) *v.* to move along smoothly or continuously

forecast (for´ kast´) *v.* to tell what may or will happen; predict

forth (forth) *adv.* forward into view

frilly (fril´ ē) *adj.* overly decorative

funnel cloud (fun´ əl kloud) *n.* the cloud at the base of a tornado that is wide at one end and thin at the other

G

gain (gān) *n.* an improvement

generates (jen´ ə rāts) *v.* to produce or cause to

guard (gard) *v.* to keep safe from harm or danger

guard

H

hazard (haz´ ûrd) *n.* a source of danger, harm, or loss

heal (hēl) *v.* to make or become healthy again

heart (hart) *n.* one's innermost feelings or spirit

hitch (hich) *n.* an unexpected delay or obstacle

homestead (hōm´ sted) *n.* a house and the farmland it is on

horizon (hə rī´ zən) *n.* the line where the earth and the sky seem to meet

horizon

huff (huf) *n.* a sudden feeling of anger, resentment, or hurt pride

I

instruments (in´ strə mənts) *n.* plural form of **instrument:** a tool, especially one designed for precise or careful work

intended (in tend´ id) *v.* a form of the verb **intend:** to mean or plan to do something

intense (in tens´) *adj.* very great or strong

intermission (in´ tûr mi´ shən) *n.* the time between events or periods of activity

international (in´ tûr na´ shə nəl) *adj.* relating to two or more countries

internment (in´ tûrn´ mənt) *n.* the process of being confined to a particular place during a time of war

Pronunciation Key: at; lāte; câre; fäther; set; mē[1]; it; kīte; ox; rōse; ô in bought; coin; bŏŏk; tōō; form; out; up; ūse; tûrn; ə sound in about, chicken, pencil cannon, circus; chair; ring; shop; thin; there; zh in treasure.

kimono (ki mō´ nō) *n.* a loose robe that is tied with a sash

lair (lâr) *n.* a home or resting place, especially of a wild animal

launch (lônch) *v.* to start something with enthusiasm

lavish (lav´ ish) *adj.* given in great amounts; more than necessary

link (lingk) *v.* to join by rings or loops; unite; connect

literate (lit´ ûr it) *adj.* able to read and write

magnificent (mag nif´ ə sənt) *adj.* very beautiful or splendid

master (mas´ tûr) *n.* a person who has great skill, ability, or knowledge in something; an expert

media (mē´ dē ə) *n.* a press or broadcasting company that communicates with large audiences

meteorologist (mē´ tē ə rol´ ə jist) *n.* an expert in the science dealing with the study of the atmosphere

meteorologist

mine (mīn) *v.* to dig in the earth

mingled (ming´ gəld) *v.* a form of the verb **mingle:** to move about freely

minimize (min´ ə mīz) *v.* to reduce to the smallest or least possible amount or degree

mirage (mi räzh´) *n.* an illusion in which an object that is seen at a distance is not really there

mobile (mō´ bəl) *adj.* capable of moving or being moved

mockingly (mok´ing lē) *adv.* in a manner that is intended to ridicule or make fun of someone or something

mutinied (mū´tə nēd) *v.* a form of the verb **mutiny:** to rebel against the person or people in charge

muttered (mu´tûrd) *v.* a form of the verb **mutter:** to speak in a low, unclear way

natives (nā´tivz) *n.* plural form of **native:** one of the original people, animals, or plants of a country or place

navigate (nav´i gāt´) *v.* to plan or direct the course of

noble (nō´bəl) *adj.* having or showing greatness; worthy

opinion (ə pin´yən) *n.* a belief based on a person's judgment rather than what is proven

order (or´dûr) *n.* a request for goods

orderly (or´dûr lē) *adj.* free from disturbance, trouble, or violence

origami (or ə go´mē) *n.* the Japanese art of folding paper into the form of an animal, flower, or other object

pack (pak) *n.* a group of animals that are alike

pack

parade (pə rād´) *v.* to walk in a way that attracts attention

parched (parcht) *adj.* very dry

pardon (par´dən) *v.* to free a person from punishment

particles (par´ti kəlz) *n.* plural form of **particle:** a very small bit or piece of something

pastime (pas´tīm) *n.* something that makes time pass pleasantly

Pronunciation Key: at; lāte; câre; fäther; set; mē; it; kīte; ox; rōse; ô in bought; coin; book; too; form; out; up; ūse; tûrn; ə sound in about, chicken, pencil cannon, circus; chair; ring; shop; thin; there; zh in treasure.

peered (pērd) *v.* a form of the verb **peer:** to look closely at something

permanent (pûr´mə nənt) *adj.* meant to last for a very long time or forever

plateaus (pla tōz´) *n.* plural form of **plateau:** an area of flat land higher than the surrounding country

poised (poizd) *v.* a form of the verb **poise:** to keep in balance

polar (pō´lûr) *adj.* having to do with the North Pole or the South Pole

precious (presh´əs) *adj.* having great value or cost

precipitation (pri sip´i tā´shən) *n.* any form of water that falls to Earth, such as rain, hail, or snow

precipitation

prepare (pri´pâr) *v.* to get ready

pressure (presh´ûr) *n.* the force that is produced by the weight of the atmosphere

pride (prīd) *n.* a sense of one's personal worth or dignity

principal (prin´sə pəl) *adj.* greatest or first, as in importance, rank, or value

professor (prə fes´ûr) *n.* a teacher at a college or university

proper (prop´ûr) *adj.* suitable, appropriate, or correct for a given purpose

prosperous (pros´pûr əs) *adj.* having success, wealth, or good fortune

prove (proov) *v.* to show the truth of

radar (rā´ dar) *n.* a device that uses reflected radio waves to track objects like aircraft, automobiles, and weather conditions

recognized (rek´ ig nīzd) *v.* a form of the verb **recognize:** to know or remember from before; identify

refreshing (ri fresh´ ing) *adj.* restoring strength or vitality; makes fresh again

reins (rānz) *n.* plural form of **rein:** a narrow strap attached to a bridle to guide and control a horse

reins

report (ri port´) *n.* a story in a newspaper or on the radio or television that gives information about something

researchers (rē´ sûrch ûrz) *n.* plural form of **researcher:** a person who carefully studies a subject to find and report new knowledge

rush (rush) *n.* the act of rushing; a sudden, swift movement

rustle (rus´ əl) *v.* to make a series of soft, fluttering sounds, as that of papers or leaves being rubbed together or stirred about

S

safari (sə far´ ē) *n.* a hunting or an investigative trip

sandbar (sand´ bar´) *n.* a built up section of sand that is near or just above the surface of the water

sandwiched (sand´ wicht) *v.* a form of the verb **sandwich:** to fit or squeeze in tightly

saplings (sap´ lingz) *n.* plural form of **sapling:** a young tree

scene (sēn) *n.* the place where an action or event occurs or occurred

seized (sēzd) *v.* a form of the verb **seize:** to grab or take hold by force

serious (sēr´ē əs) *adj.* causing concern or anxiety; dangerous

severe (sə vēr) *adj.* harsh; causing hardship or discomfort

sod (sod) *n.* a cut layer of soil with grass growing on it

sod

spindly (spind´lē) *adj.* having a tall, slender shape

spirit (spēr´it) *n.* a supernatural being or essence

spread (spred) *v.* to extend over an area

sputtered (spu´tûrd) *v.* a form of the verb **sputter:** to speak quickly in a confused way

stables (stā´bəlz) *n.* plural form of **stable:** a building, especially one with stalls, where horses or cattle are kept and fed

startling (star´təl ing´) *adj.* surprising or frightening

straight (strāt) *adv.* in one direction without changing or bending

strike (strīk) *v.* to find suddenly or unexpectedly

surge (sûrj) *n.* a sudden increase or rise

sweep (swēp) *v.* to move, bring, or carry with a swift movement

sweltered (swel´tûrd) *v.* a form of the verb **swelter:** to suffer, sweat, or become faint from heat

swished (swisht) *v.* a form of the verb **swish:** to move with a soft, muffled sound

symbolized (sim´bəl īzd´) *v.* a form of the verb **symbolize:** to be or serve as a symbol for something else; to represent

tasted (tāst´ id) *v.* a form of the verb **taste:** to get the flavor of something

temperamental (tem´ pûr men´ təl) *adj.* showing moodiness, sensitivity, or irritability

tended (ten´ did) *v.* a form of the verb **tend:** to take care of

territory (târ´ i tor´ ē) *n.* land and water under the control of a government

threat (thret) *n.* a sign or possibility that something dangerous or unfortunate may happen

throughout (throo out´) *prep.* in every part of

thrust (thrust) *v.* to push with force

tie (tī) *n.* a part of a structure that holds together or strengthens other parts

ties

timeless (tīm´ les) *adj.* unaffected by the passage of time; eternal

toward (tword) *prep.* in the direction of

trade (trād) *v.* to engage in buying and selling

transmit (tranz mit´) *v.* to communicate

treaty (trē´ tē) *n.* a formal agreement, especially between nations

tropics (trop´ iks) *n.* a region of Earth near the equator where it is always warm

trudged (trujd) *v.* a form of the verb **trudge:** to walk slowly and with effort

tundra (tun´ drə) *n.* flat, treeless land of permanently frozen soil and little vegetation

tundra

459

unique (ū nēk´) *adj.* highly unusual or noteworthy; remarkable

unselfish (un´ sel´ fish) *adj.* thinking of others

updraft (up´ draft) *n.* an upward current of air

vapor (vā´ pûr) *n.* small particles of mist, steam, or smoke that can be seen in the air

warbler (wor´ blûr) *n.* a small songbird with bright colors

waste (wāst) *v.* to spend or use foolishly

whirlpool (wûrl´ pool) *n.* a current of water or air that moves very fast in a circle

yards (yardz) *n.* plural form of **yard:** a measure of length equal to 36 inches, or 3 feet

yoke (yōk) *n.* a wooden frame consisting of a long, curved bar fitted with two hoops by which two work animals are joined

yoke

Reading Resources

Reading Comprehension

Comprehension Strategies will help you understand what you are reading.

Asking and Answering Questions

As you read, ask yourself the following questions:

1. What do I already know about this topic?

2. What else would I like to know about this topic?

3. What questions do I think the author will answer as I read this selection?

4. How does this information connect to what I already know about the topic?

5. How does this information connect to the unit theme?

6. What is not making sense in this selection?

7. What is interfering with my understanding?

8. How does this information answer my question?

9. Does this information completely answer my question?

10. Do I have more questions after finding some of my answers?

11. Can I skim the text in order to find an answer to my question?

Clarifying

As you read, ask yourself the following questions:

1. What does not make sense? If it is a word, how can I figure it out? Do I use context clues, word analysis, or apposition, or do I need to ask someone or look it up in the dictionary or glossary?

2. If a sentence is complicated, have I reread it as well as the sentences around it to see if the meaning is clarified? Have I read the sentence part by part to see exactly what is confusing? Have I tried to restate the sentence in my own words?

3. The paragraph is long and full of details. What can I do to understand it? How much will I need to slow down to make sure I understand the text? Do I need to back up and reread part of the text to understand it?

4. Do I need to take notes or discuss what I have just read in order to understand it?

5. What is the main idea of what I just read?

6. Can I put what I just read into my own words?

Making Connections

As you read, ask yourself the following questions:

1. What does this remind me of? What else have I read like this?

2. How does this connect with something in my own life?

3. How does this connect with other selections I have read?

4. How does this connect with what is going on in the world today?

5. How does this relate to other events or topics I have studied in social studies or science?

Predicting

As you read, ask yourself the following questions:

1. What clues in the text can help me predict what will happen next?

2. What clues in the text tell me what probably will not happen next?

Revising/Confirming Predictions

As you read, ask yourself the following questions:

1. How was my prediction confirmed?

2. Why was my prediction *not* confirmed?

3. What clues did I miss that would have helped me make a better prediction?

Summarizing

As you read, ask yourself the following questions:

1. What is this selection about?

2. What are the big ideas the writer is trying to get at?

3. Have I said the same thing more than once in my summary?

4. What can I delete from my summary? What is not important?

5. How can I put what I have just read into my own words?

Visualizing

As you read, ask yourself the following questions:

1. What picture do the words create in my mind? What specific words help create feelings, actions, and settings in my mind?

2. What can I see, hear, smell, taste, and/or feel in my mind?

3. How does this picture help me understand what I am reading?

4. How does my mental picture extend beyond the words in the text?

Accessing Complex Text Skills will help you understand the purpose and organization of a selection.

Cause and Effect

Cause-and-effect relationships help you understand connections between the events in a story. The cause is why something happens. The effect is what happens as a result. A cause produces an effect.

Classify and Categorize

An author often includes many details in a story. Putting the like things together, or classifying those like things into categories, helps you see how actions, events, and characters from a story are related.

Compare and Contrast

To compare means to tell how things, events, or characters are alike. To contrast means to tell how things, events, or characters are different. Writers compare and contrast to make an idea clearer or to make a story more interesting.

Fact and Opinion

Writers often use facts and opinions in their writing to make their writing more believable, to explain things, or to persuade readers. A fact is a statement that can be proven true. An opinion is something a person or a group feels or believes is true, though others may disagree. Opinions are not necessarily true.

Main Idea and Details

The main idea is what the story or paragraph is mostly about. Writers use details to tell more about or explain the main idea.

Making Inferences

You make inferences when you take information in the selection about a character or an event and add this information to what you already know. You can use this combination of information to make a statement or conclusion about that character or event.

Sequence

Sequence is the order in which things happen in a story. The more you know about the sequence of events in a story, the better you will understand the story. Writers use time and order words such as *first, then, finally, tonight,* and *yesterday* to tell the order of events.

Writer's Craft

Author's Purpose

Everything is written for a purpose. That purpose may be to entertain, to persuade, or to inform. Knowing why a piece is written—what purpose the author had for writing the piece—gives the reader an idea of what to expect and perhaps some prior idea of what the author is going to say. It is possible for an author to have more than one purpose.

Character

A character is a person or creature that interacts with others within a story. There are different kinds of characters in stories, and different ways to describe them. Readers learn to identify the different characteristics of the characters (physical features, character types such as heroes or villains, personality types, feelings, and motivations), and the ways the author describes the characters, such as with descriptive details, dialogue, and illustrations.

Genre Knowledge

Readers learn to recognize the differences between fiction and nonfiction. Subgenres of fiction include realistic fiction, fantasy, fairy tales, folktales, plays, and poems. Subgenres of nonfiction include informational texts, biographies, and reference books. Readers determine which features are used for these different subgenres.

Language Use

Readers learn to recognize the ways authors communicate important details and events in a story. Language use may include rhyme, repetition, sentence structures (simple, compound, declarative, interrogative, imperative, and exclamatory), alliteration, simile, metaphor, exaggeration, onomatopoeia, personification, sensory details, descriptive words, effective adjectives and adverbs, dialogue, and formal vs. informal language.

Plot

Readers learn to recognize the overall structure, or plot, of a story. A plot usually includes a beginning, a problem that must be solved, the climax or highest point of the story, a resolution of the problem, and an ending. Authors may use sequence, cause and effect, details, and dialogue to build the plot.

Point of View (Narrative/Fiction)

Point of view in a narrative involves identifying who is telling the story. If a character in a narrative is telling the story, that character uses his or her point of view to describe the action in the story and tell about the other characters. This is called first-person point of view. If the narrative is told in third-person point of view, someone outside the story who is aware of all the characters' thoughts, feelings, and actions is relating them to the reader.

Point of View (Informational or Persuasive Text)

The author's point of view in an informational text is the position or perspective the author takes on the subject he or she is writing about. The author may arrange topics in a certain sequence, or the author might present facts in such a way as to inform or to persuade his or her audience.

Setting

The setting of a story is composed of three pieces: the place where the story occurs, the timeframe or when the story takes place, and the amount of time that passes within the story from the beginning to the end.

Text Features

Text features are usually used in informational texts, and they help readers make sense of what they are reading. Text features may include headings, illustrations, photos, captions, diagrams, charts, maps, punctuation, font size or color, and numbered or bulleted lists.

Vocabulary Strategies

Apposition

Sometimes the word is defined within the text. In apposition, the word is followed by the definition, which is set off by commas.

Context Clues

When you come to an unfamiliar word in your reading, look for clues in the sentence or in the surrounding sentences. These clues might help you understand the meaning of the word.

Word Analysis

Examining the parts of a word can help you figure out the word's meaning. For example, the word *unfriendly* can be broken down into word parts: the prefix *un-*, the base word *friend,* and the suffix *-ly.* Knowing the meaning of each part will help you come up with the definition "not friendly."

Comprehension Discussion Strategies

Asking and Answering Questions

1. What if . . .
2. How do we know . . .
3. I wonder what would happen if . . .
4. What do we know about . . .
5. I wonder why the author chose to . . .
6. I found I could skim the material because . . .

Clarifying

1. I have a question about . . .
2. I am still confused about . . .
3. Does anyone know . . .
4. Could we clarify . . .
5. I figured out that . . .
6. I had difficulty understanding _____ because . . .
7. I still do not understand . . .
8. What did the author mean when he or she wrote _____?
9. Who can help me clarify _____ ?
10. Why did the author _____?
11. I decided to read this more slowly because . . .

Making Connections

1. This made me think . . .
2. I was reminded of . . .
3. This selection reminds me of what we read in _____ because . . .
4. This selection connects to the unit theme because . . .
5. I would like to make a connection to . . .
6. I found _____ interesting because . . .

7. This author's writing reminds me of . . .

Predicting

1. I expect . . .

2. I predict . . .

3. Based on _____, I predict . . .

4. I can support my prediction by/with . . .

5. I would like to change my prediction because . . .

6. My prediction was confirmed when/by . . .

7. My prediction was not confirmed because . . .

Summarizing

1. I think the main idea is . . .

2. I think an important supporting detail is . . .

3. I think the best evidence to support the main idea is . . .

4. To summarize . . .

5. I learned . . .

6. I can conclude . . .

Visualizing

1. When I read _____, I visualized . . .

2. The author's words _____ helped me visualize . . .

3. Visualizing helped me understand . . .

4. The author made the story really come alive by . . .

Collaborative Conversation Starters

Personal Response

1. I did not know that . . . .

2. I liked the part where . . . .

3. I agree with _____ because . . . .

4. I disagree with _____ because . . . .

5. The reason I think _____ is . . .

6. I was surprised to find out . . .

7. I like the way the author developed the character by . . .

Agreeing with a Response

1. I agree because . . .

2. I see what you mean because . . .

Disagreeing with a Response

1. I disagree because . . .

2. I think we can agree that _____, but . . .

Rules for Collaborative Conversation

Speaking Rules

☐ Speak clearly.

☐ Speak at an appropriate pace.

☐ Stay on topic.

☐ Use appropriate language for the setting.

☐ Make eye contact with the audience.

Listening Rules

☐ Look at the person who is speaking.

☐ Respect speakers by listening attentively.

☐ Keep your hands still and in your lap when someone is speaking.

☐ Do not talk when someone else is speaking.

☐ When you want to say something, raise your hand and wait to be called on.

☐ Ask a question if you do not understand something you heard.

Discussion Rules

☐ Listen carefully as others speak.

☐ Do not interrupt a speaker.

☐ Raise your hand when you want to speak.

☐ Ask questions to get more information from a speaker.

☐ Keep quiet as others speak.

☐ Take turns speaking.

☐ Respond to questions that others have asked you.

☐ Keep your questions and responses focused on the item being discussed.

Photo Credits

Front Cover (roller coaster perched over city)Oliver Burston/Ikon Images/Getty Images, (rocket)goktugg/E+/Getty Images; **viii** (t)Loren M Rye/Getty Images, (c)©Doug Sherman/Geofile; **ix** (c)©Tom Wang/Alamy; **x** (c)©John Springer Collection/Corbis; **xi** (t)Prints & Photographs Online Catalog, Library of Congress, LC-USZ62-104378, (c)Frank Carter/Getty Images; **9** imageBROKER/Alamy; **10-11** val lawless/iStock/Getty Images; **11** (tl)Bananastock/age fotostock, (tr)KidStock/Blend Images/Getty Images, (br)JUPITERIMAGES/Brand X/Alamy; **53** Robert Churchill/Alamy; **74-75** Prints & Photographs Division, Library of Congress, LC-DIG-pga-01018; **76** ©Corbis; **82-83** cbpix/Alamy; **113** Michael Bodmann/Getty Images; **156-157** George Doyle/Getty Images; **157** (tl)Dean Mitchell/Stock/Getty Images, (tr)Jupiterimages/Photos.com/Getty Images, (br)MamiGibbs/Moment/Getty Images; **158-159** ©2010 Willoughby Owen/Getty Images; **160** Loren M Rye/Getty Images; **161** Ryan McGinnis/Alamy; **162** Purestock/SuperStock; **163** (l)Timothy Bethke/Alamy, (r)Melody Ovard, OMAO/NOAA Ship Nancy Foster, NOAA/Department of Commerce; **164** Ryan McGinnis/Alamy; **165** NWS WFO, Norman OK/NOAA; **166** bildagentur-online.com/th-foto/Alamy; **167** Ryan McGinnis/Getty Images; **168** ©Ryan McGinnis/Alamy; **169** Ryan McGinnis/age fotostock; **170** Skip ODonnell/Getty Images; **171** iStockphoto/Getty Images; **172** Loren M Rye/Getty Images; **178-179** Fotosearch/Getty Images; **179** (tl)Don Paulson Photography/Purestock/SuperStock, (tr)Exactostock/SuperStock, (bl)Photo by Roger Hill, USDA Natural Resources Conservation Service, (br)Don Paulson Photography/Purestock/SuperStock; **180** (tr)©Ariel Skelley/Blend Images LLC, (cl)©Ingram Publishing/SuperStock, (cr)Realistic Reflections, (br)Image Source/Isadora Getty Buyou; **181** ©Corbis Premium RF/Alamy; **183** Johner Images/Alamy; **184** ©Doug Sherman/Geofile; **186** Best View Stock/Getty Images; **187** Gabriel Carlson/iStock/Getty Images Plus; **189** Jim Tampin/Alamy; **190** Don Paulson Photography/Purestock/SuperStock; **192** KariannE/Stockimo/Alamy; **193** (t)Pixtal/age fotostock, (cl)©Doug Sherman/Geofile, (cr)Kenneth Wiedemann/Getty Images, (b)Ingmar Wesemann/Getty Images; **194-195** Photo by Tim McCabe, USDA Natural Resources Conservation Service; **196** (l)©Ingram Publishing/SuperStock, (r)©Ariel Skelley/Blend Images LLC; **223** Ilene MacDonald/Alamy; **234** Squaredpixels/E+/Getty Images; **235** Vladimir Isaakjan/Alamy; **241** Sergio Pitamitz/Getty Images; **242-243** Tom Wang/Alamy; **244-245** Ingram Publishing; **246** Fuse/Getty Images; **247** mtcurado/iStockphoto/Getty Images; **249** Bryan Mullennix/Getty Images; **250-251** HIT1912/iStockphoto/Getty Images; **252** (l)stevegeer/iStockphoto/Getty Images, (t)Donald E. Hall/Getty Images, (r)Mark Conlin/Alamy; **253** Doug James/Alamy; **254** (l)William Perry/iStockphoto/Getty Images, (inset)Robert Hamilton/Alamy Stock Photo; **255** alacatr/iStock/Getty Images Plus; **256** Volodymyr Goinyk/iStockphoto/Getty Images; **257** Ingram Publishing; **258** MQ Naufal/Alamy; **259** Uwe Halstenbach/iStockphoto/Getty Images; **260** Donald E. Hall/Getty Images; **265** (l)Ralph Lee Hopkins/Getty Images, (r)Lissa Harrison; **312-313** chrisdeana/iStock/Getty Images; **313** (tl)Buyenlarge/Archive Photos/Getty Images, (tr)Spaces Images/Blend Images/Getty Images, (br)Thinkstock images/Stockbyte/Getty images; **331** (l)©Tetra Images/SuperStock, (r)Purestock/SuperStock; **332-333** ©Bettmann/Corbis; **334** Prints & Photographs Online Catalog, Library of Congress, LC-USW3-023967-D; **335** Gilles Petard/Contributor/Getty Images; **336-337** Prints & Photographs Online Catalog, Library of Congress, LC-USZ62-15236; **337** Prints & Photographs Online Catalog, Library of Congress, LC-USF34-040820-D; **338** Prints & Photographs Online Catalog, Library of Congress, LC-DIG-det-4a23082; **339** Prints & Photographs Online Catalog, Library of Congress, LC-USF34-T01-009133-C; **340** Prints & Photographs Online Catalog, Library of Congress, LC-DIG-fsa-8d28514; **341** ©Corbis; **342** (l)Library of Congress, Prints and Photographs Division [LC-USZ62-62394], (r)Prints & Photographs Online Catalog, Library of Congress, LC-USZ62-42529; **343** (l)Prints & Photographs Online Catalog, Library of Congress, LC-USZC4-13592, (r)Photo by Museum of the City of New York/Getty Images; **344** Underwood Photo Archives/SuperStock; **345** Prints & Photographs Online Catalog, Library of Congress, LC-USZ62-137893; **346** Prints & Photographs Online Catalog, Library of Congress, LC-USZ62-123107; **346-347** ©John Springer Collection/Corbis; **348** Prints & Photographs Online Catalog, Library of Congress LC-USF33-T01-002049-M3; **348-349** STOCK4B-RF/Glow Images; **349** Prints and Photographs Division, Library of Congress, LC-USZ62-43605; **350** Prints & Photographs Online Catalog, Library of Congress, LC-USZ62-123107; **374-375** Prints & Photographs Online Catalog, Library of Congress, LC-USZ62-116721; **376** JamesTung/iStockphoto/Getty Images; **378** Prints & Photographs Online Catalog, Library of Congress, LC-USZ62-104378; **380** Frank Tozier/Alamy; **380-381** Prints & Photographs Division, Library of Congress, LC-USZC4-2566; **381** Prints & Photographs Online Catalog, Library of Congress, LC-USZ62-115659; **383** amana images inc./Alamy; **384-385** Design Pics/Richard Wear; **386** Prints & Photographs Division, Library of Congress, LC-USZC4-2566; **391** (l)Popular Graphic Arts, Library of Congress, LC-USZC4-12427, (r)Jonathan A. Meyers/Science Source; **396** Genthe Collection, Library of Congress, LC-G397-T-0347; **397** Stereograph Cards, Library of Congress, LC-USZ62-122784; **398** ©Bettmann/Corbis; **399** (l)National Archives and Records Administration, (r)National Archives and Records Administration; **400-401** National Archives and Records Administration; **401** National Archives and Records Administration; **404** Museum of the City of New York/Byron Collection/Getty Images; **405** Frank Carter/Getty Images; **406** National Archives and Records Administration; **411** K-King Photography Media Co. Ltd/Getty Images; **447** U.S. Fish & Wildlife Service; **449** Ken Welsh/age fotostock; **450** ©Ingram Publishing/SuperStock; **451** Alexey Stiop/Getty Images; **452** Juice Images/Alamy; **453** (l)Anderson Ross/Alamy, (r)STOCK4B-RF/Glow Images; **454** Image Source/Getty Images; **455** ©image100/Corbis; **456** olaser/Getty Images; **457** ©mylife photos/Alamy; **458** Allison Herreid/Getty Images; **459** (l)Ei Katsumata/Alamy, (r)ajliikala/Getty Images; **460** apCincy/Getty Images; **Back Cover** (roller coaster perched over city)Oliver Burston/Ikon Images/Getty Images, (rocket)goktugg/E+/Getty Images.